The Books the Church Suppressed

Fiction and truth in The Da Vinci Code

The Books the Church Suppressed

Fiction and truth in The Da Vinci Code

Michael Green

MONARCH
BOOKS

Oxford, UK & Grand Rapids, Michigan, USA

First published in the UK in 2005 by Monarch Books
(a publishing imprint of Lion Hudson plc),
Mayfield House, 256 Banbury Road, Oxford, OX2 7DH
Tel: +44 (0) 1865 302750 Fax: +44 (0) 1865 302757

ISBN-13: 978-1-85424-698-1 (UK)
ISBN-10: 1-85424-698-4 (UK)
ISBN-13: 978-0-8254-6096-8 (USA)
ISBN-10: 0-8254-6096-4 (USA)

Distributed by:
UK: Marston Book Services Ltd, PO Box 269,
Abingdon, Oxon OX14 4YN
USA: Kregel Publications, PO Box 2607,
Grand Rapids, Michigan 49501
Worldwide co-edition produced by Lion Hudson plc,
Mayfield House, 256 Banbury Road, Oxford, OX2 7DH
Tel: +44 (0) 1865 302750 Fax: +44 (0) 1865 302757

Unless otherwise stated, all Scripture quotations are from the
Revised Standard Version of the Bible, © 1946, 1952, 1973, Division of
Christian Education of the National Council of the Churches of Christ in
the United States of America. Used by permission. All rights reserved.

British Library Cataloguing Data
A catalogue record for this book is available
from the British Library.

Printed in Great Britain.

Contents

For my gifted friend, the Revd Lee McMunn
and his generation of scholar-preachers and apologists

Chapter One

The books the church suppressed?

ne of the most celebrated blockbusters in recent times has been Dan Brown's *The Da Vinci Code*. Published in 2003, the book has been translated into more than 40 languages, boasts more than 7 million copies in hardback alone, and has been at or near the top of the best-seller lists in major Western countries for more than a year. A film of the book is to be launched in 2006. The book has attracted an enormous amount of publicity. This is not only because it is a superb thriller, but also because of its sub-plot, which has a mixture of suspense, sensuality, spiritual search, superstition and revived paganism, while it sets out to under-mine the credibility of the New Testament, the divinity of Christ and the witness of the church, particularly the Roman Catholic Church. "What I mean," says Teabing, the chief pro-tagonist of Brown's sub-plot, "is that almost everything our fathers taught about Christ is false."

What, then, is this revolutionary re-evaluation of Christianity? Stripped of the beguiling charm of his prose, the following are Brown's main points. The first two are closely intertwined.

Brown asserts that Jesus was not divine, and was never thought to be until the Council of Nicaea in 325 AD, when the matter was put to the vote and just scraped through. It was there, according to Teabing, "that many aspects of Christianity were debated and voted upon", including "the divinity of Jesus".

9

Sophie Neveu, the cryptologist to whom Teabing propounds this theory, is shocked. "I don't follow. His divinity?"

"My dear," said Teabing, "until *that* moment in history Jesus was viewed by His followers as a mortal prophet ... a great and powerful man, but a *man* nonetheless. A mortal."

"Not the Son of God?"

"Right," Teabing said. "Jesus' establishment as 'the Son of God' was officially proposed and voted on by the Council of Nicaea."

"Hold on. You're saying Jesus' divinity was the result of a *vote*?"

"A relatively close vote at that," Teabing replies.

He goes on to argue that this was all a clever move on the part of the Emperor Constantine (c. 274–337 AD), the date of whose conversion to Christianity is uncertain. Brown is wrong in maintaining that he was not a Christian until the end of his life, though it is true that he deferred baptism until his deathbed, like many in those days. His letters from 313 onwards leave no doubt that he saw himself as a Christian. Brown rightly discerns that Constantine was concerned to consolidate his power in the world. He had decreed that Christianity should become the faith of the Empire. Brown argues that he was concerned to upgrade the status of Jesus from mere mortal (as Brown thinks he had been regarded for the past three centuries) to that of Son of God. "To rewrite the history books, Constantine knew he would need a bold stroke. From this sprang the most profound moment in Christian history ... Constantine commissioned and financed a new Bible, which omitted those gospels that spoke of Christ's *human* traits and embellished those gospels that made Him godlike. The earlier gospels were outlawed, gathered up and burned."

Brown continues: "Fortunately for historians ... some of

the gospels that Constantine attempted to eradicate managed to survive. The Dead Sea Scrolls were found in the 1950s hidden in a cave near Qumran in the Judaean desert. And, of course, the Coptic Scrolls in 1945 at Nag Hammadi. In addition to telling the true Grail story, these documents speak of Christ's ministry in very human terms ... The scrolls highlight glaring historical discrepancies and fabrications, clearly confirming that the modern Bible was compiled and edited by men who possessed a political agenda – to promote the divinity of the man Jesus Christ and use His influence to solidify their own power base."

Before we go any further, it is important to be quite clear what is being claimed. It is nothing less than this, that the whole collection of books that go to make our New Testament were selected by Constantine in the fourth century to serve his political agenda.

There would have to be some very good evidence to support so radical a solution. Later in the book we shall examine that evidence.

In order to maintain such a thesis, even for a moment, Brown has to rubbish the New Testament documents. This he does by maintaining that they are secondary to the Coptic Gnostic gospels found at Nag Hammadi in Egypt (we examine the nature of Gnosticism in subsequent chapters). He writes: "More than *eighty* gospels were considered for the New Testament, and yet only a relative few were chosen for inclusion – Matthew, Mark, Luke and John among them." In due course we will have to look carefully at the date and contents of these Gnostic gospels, as well as at the nature of Gnosticism. But for the moment we want to get Brown's position clear. It is entirely dependent on the validity, reliability and very early date of the Gnostic gospels. The whole position adopted by this book, and several like it, rests on these

Gnostic gospels. "These are photocopies of the Nag Hammadi and Dead Sea Scrolls, which I mentioned earlier," Teabing said. "The earliest Christian records. Troublingly they do not match up with the gospels in the Bible." Flipping to the middle of a book entitled *The Gnostic Gospels*, Teabing pointed to a passage. "*The Gospel of Philip* is always a good place to start."

The passage reads: "And the companion of the Saviour is Mary Magdalene. Christ loved her more than all the disciples and used to kiss her often on her mouth. The rest of the disciples were offended by it and expressed disapproval. They said to him, 'Why do you love her more than all of us?'"

Sophie is not convinced. "It says nothing of marriage," she says. Teabing responds: "As any Aramaic scholar will tell you, the word companion, in those days, literally meant spouse." That of course is not a very helpful comment, even in a novel like this, since the passage occurs only in Coptic and has nothing to do with Aramaic!

Unworried by this, Teabing – and of course Brown behind him – goes on to make the major claim, namely that Jesus loved Mary Magdalene and married her; a fact, we are told, that has been "explored ad nauseam by modern historians". Mary Magdalene is seen not only as the wife of Jesus but as the mother of his child – whose dynasty still survives in France. Teabing then cites a phrase from *The Gospel of Mary Magdalene* to the effect that Jesus had given revelations to Mary which he had not shared with the male disciples. In the passage Peter is indignant: "Did the Saviour really speak with a woman without our knowledge? Are we to turn about and all listen to her?" Brown concludes that Jesus gave instructions to Mary Magdalene about the future of his church, not to Simon Peter. She was to lead it. Jesus, the argument runs, was the original feminist. The legend of the Holy Grail does not concern the chalice at the Last Supper, but the womb of

Mary Magdalene. She "was the Holy Vessel ... the chalice that bore the royal bloodline of Jesus Christ."

Enough of *The Da Vinci Code*, for the moment. It is, after all, only a novel, alive with unsubstantiated claim and innuendo, but nevertheless fascinating. But it is full of historical errors, which Dan Brown refuses to acknowledge or discuss. For example, the documents from which he draws are at least two hundred years later than the New Testament. There is no shred of evidence anywhere that Jesus married Mary Magdalene, let alone that they had a child. It is obvious to anyone reading the earliest parts of the New Testament, such as Philippians 2:4-10 that the author, a converted Jew, writing in the first half of the first century, is passionately convinced of the deity of Jesus, as are all the New Testament writers and the apostolic Fathers who follow them. The deity as well as the humanity of Jesus was not dreamed up at Nicaea, but was the unique conviction which from the apostolic age onwards set Christianity on a collision course with Rome's edict that the emperor should be worshipped as divine. It was primarily their refusal to worship the emperor that cost the early Christians such fierce persecution. So, far from the deity of Jesus being first formulated at Nicaea, all but two of the assembled bishops assembled from all over the Empire at that Council upheld the three-centuries-old Christian conviction on this point in the face of some dilution proposed by an attractive heretic, Arius. Constantine did not outlaw and burn the Gnostic gospels, which had long been spurned by the church. They were left to wither on the vine. But he did finance the publication of 50 Bibles for the churches in Constantinople, two of which may possibly survive today in the fourth-century manuscripts Sinaiticus and Vaticanus.

Needless to say, there were not "more than eighty

gospels" competing for inclusion in the New Testament – that sounds good but is pure fiction. The true situation will become apparent in a later chapter. And the idea that the Dead Sea Scrolls have anything to do with Christianity is ludicrous, and is maintained by no reputable scholar – although the Scrolls do much to illuminate the background into which Christianity came. The plain fact is that the latest of them was written well before Jesus' birth!

The main purpose of this anti-Christian sub-plot in Brown's book is twofold. He wants to make the case for a revival of paganism, which embraces the "sacred feminine" and is superior to Christianity, seen as male-dominated and hierarchical. That is a very seductive thesis these days. But it must be noted that the "sacred feminine" is much broader than the *hieros gamos* or sexual union which is a secret part of the plot. It is very much the goddess Gaia concept of New Age thought. In modern clothing it is naturalism, to which the human heart always tends to return once it rejects divine revelation and rescue. For in New Age thought the feminine does not stand for a personal being but rather for the life-giving and creative principle within this world. And this world is all there is. The universe is one, and everything in it shares the same essential nature, people and rats, trees and rocks. All is one, creativity comes from within, and there is no God outside the universe. Such is the ideology of Monism, as much present in Brown's book as it is in Eastern Hindu thought. It is attractive to many today.

But Brown has a second purpose, not only to advance the feminist principle of paganism, but to attack Christianity directly. In order to do this he has to undermine the authority of the New Testament records. As we have seen, he does so by making use of the Gnostic gospels. So does the film *The Last Temptation of Christ*. So does the book which itself was a blockbuster a decade and more ago, *The Holy Blood and The Holy Grail*, written by Michael Baigent, Richard Leigh and Henry Lincoln, on whose plot Brown draws extensively. We shall have to see how well this belief in the early date of the Gnostic gospels stands up to critical evaluation. But the question that presents itself first of all is, where do these novelists derive their ideas from?

Many will have heard of the Jesus Seminar. Composed largely of American scholars on the fringe of New Testament Studies, it meets to discuss the sayings of Jesus one by one, and then votes on their authenticity, by casting different-coloured marbles into a bowl. They are given four options: certainly authentic, probably authentic, certainly inauthentic and probably inauthentic. The project is laughable. How can you decide highly complex issues like these (debated by scholars for over two hundred years) by throwing a marble into a bowl two thousand years after the events in question? The Seminar is generally a laughing stock in serious New Testament circles. However, now and again an interesting theory emerges. John Dominic Crossan is one of the brightest of this group, and he goes against almost every scholar in the world by surmising that one of the books found at Nag Hammadi, the *Gospel of Thomas*, a collection of "sayings of Jesus" (some of which are obviously Gnostic) is one of our earliest sources – earlier than any of our Gospels.

He also believes in "Q", a hypothetical document supposed to lie behind some of the sayings of Jesus that are common to Matthew and Luke. Some scholars believe it was an oral source, some a written one, and some do not believe in it at all. Crossan does, and he thinks he can detect which bits of it are earliest. Curiously enough, they just happen to look rather like bits of the *Gospel of Thomas*! Naturally, therefore, Crossan is happy to argue that our Gospels are unreliable and secondary. They misrepresent Jesus and make him a much more Jewish figure than the Gnostic teacher that Crossan deems him to be.

Then there is Professor Elaine Pagels from Princeton University. Her attractively written book *The Gnostic Gospels* introduced these writings to a much larger public than the specialists who had studied the Nag Hammadi find. She admits that these books were regarded as heretical by the church, but maintains that Christianity was so fluid in the early centuries that the whole idea of orthodoxy as opposed to heresy did not originate until the fourth century. As Teabing expresses it in *The Da Vinci Code*, "anyone who chose the forbidden gospels over Constantine's version was deemed a heretic. The word *heretic* derives from that moment in history". So Elaine Pagels raises an important question about the contents of the New Testament canon. "Who made that selection, and for what reasons? Why were these other writings excluded and banned as heresy?" Good question. We shall need to look into it.

A rather similar position is put forward by Harvard Professor Karen King, who wrote *The Gospel of Mary of Magdala: Jesus and the First Woman Apostle*. She does not believe that the first Christians had a firm core of beliefs. On the contrary, she regards the Gnostic documents as invaluable evidence of the wide spectrum of beliefs current in early Christianity. Theological diversity was the norm, she maintains – ignoring important studies to the contrary such as J.D.G. Dunn's *Unity and Diversity in the New Testament* and Martin Hengel's *The Four Gospels and the One Gospel of Jesus Christ*.

Crossan, King and Pagels are serious scholars and, although most of their colleagues remain profoundly unpersuaded by their views, they do provide the intellectual background from which the more blockbusting films and books draw. They have shown that in their support of the Gnostic gospels that there is a case to answer. Why our four Gospels and no others? Why were the Gnostic writings suppressed, or left to wither on the vine? On what principles was the collection of books that we call the canon constructed? Is there important information about Jesus which was excluded from the New Testament? These are some of the issues that need to be addressed in the chapters that follow. Perhaps we would be wise to begin by examining where the idea of a canon of sacred books came from.

Chapter Two

A Canon of Scripture - Where Did the Idea Come From?

From the earliest days of the Christian community, the Old Testament had been regarded as authoritative for the faith and practice of the people of God. Those were in the first instance Jews, but very soon the Christian faith extended far beyond Judaism and was to be found, within 30 years of the death of Jesus, in places as far afield as Alexandria, Rome, Greece and Syria as well as Palestine.

The important thing to understand is that nobody decided, "Let's have a new list of authoritative books". They already had one, in the Law, the Prophets and the Writings, the three divisions of the Hebrew Bible. The actual date of the final definition of the Hebrew Bible is disputed. It cannot have been later than about 85 AD at the Council of Jamnia, when the rabbis reflected intensively on the contents of the Hebrew Bible. Many scholars believe it long preceded that. It is clear that the first five books of the Bible, the Pentateuch, which was the first part of the Old Testament canon (or list of authoritative books), was complete and universally recognised among Jews by the time of Ezra and Nehemiah in the fifth century BC. It may have been so regarded considerably earlier. The second and third sections of the Old Testament canon, the Prophets and the Writings, were probably organised in their separate sections around 165 BC. The Syrian persecutor Antiochus Epiphanes was intensely hostile to the Jews and their Scriptures, and, after he had astonishingly been defeated in the Maccabaean war of liberation, we read that Judas Maccabaeus "collected all the books that had been lost on account of the war which had come upon us, and they are still in our possession" (2 Maccabees 2:14). The books were not, of course, between one cover at this stage. It was a collection of highly prized scrolls that Judas Maccabaeus brought together. By the beginning of the Christian era the books of the Hebrew Bible were just as we have them, and the Jewish author Josephus, writing towards the end of the first century AD, says they had all been accepted as canonical from time immemorial. His words are worth quoting:

> We do not possess myriads of inconsistent books, conflicting with each other. Our books, those which are justly accredited, are but two and twenty.

Josephus is referring to the way the Jewish Scriptures were arranged. Most Jewish reckoning saw 24 books, but Josephus is counting Lamentations as an appendix to Jeremiah and Ruth to Judges. The total of 22 may have been arranged so as to correspond with the number of letters in the Hebrew alphabet, a very Jewish touch. Significantly, Josephus continues:

> Although such long ages have now passed, no one has ventured either to add or to remove or to alter a syllable. (Josephus, *Against Apion*, 1:36ff.)

What seems to have happened at the Council of Jamnia in 85 AD was the pruning-out of certain apocryphal books which had been read alongside the acknowledged scriptures by Jews in Alexandria and Qumran.

Be that as it may, there is no doubt that the Jews, and the early Christians after them, were what the Qur'an repeatedly calls them, "people of the book". The Jews had long revered their sacred books. Jesus had displayed precisely the same attitude, and the first Christians, all initially Jewish converts, naturally adopted the Old Testament Scriptures as their own. Very soon, particularly when the Christian faith spread into Greek-speaking lands in the middle of the first century, it became plain that they found Hebrew more and more difficult, and favoured the Septuagint, the Greek translation of the Old Testament that had been written in Alexandria some time earlier.

Alexander the Great founded the city of Alexandria in 331 BC, and soon there was a substantial and growing Jewish element in this Greek city. Alexander's successors in Egypt, the Ptolemies, made Alexandria the capital of their empire – which included Judaea. So the importance of Alexandria was obvious. And it was not long before the Jews in the city gave up using the Hebrew language of their forefathers, and spoke only Greek like everyone else. To meet their needs, a Greek translation of the Hebrew Bible came into being some time in the third century BC, beginning with the Law, which was particularly important for synagogue worship. But this account of the translation was far too pedestrian for the legend! The earliest version of the legend, found in the *Letter of Aristeas*, tells us that 70 or 72 (hence the name "Septuagint", from the Latin word for 70) elders came from Jerusalem to do the translation – which took 72 days! Philo, a distinguished Alexandrian Jew who lived at the time of Jesus, embellishes the legend. The translators worked in total isolation from each other, but wrote the same text, word for word "as though it was dictated to each by an invisible prompter".

Legend though it is, it shows their profound sense that

God inspired the Scriptures. And this conviction is found in every strand of Judaism, and was strongly reinforced by Jesus himself. It is perhaps worth noting that it was only the books of the Law that the translators from Judaea put into Greek. The rest of the Old Testament was translated by the early Christians. They made this Greek work very much their own Bible. They saw it as predicting in prophecy, typology and allegory the coming, the death and the victory of Jesus. They believed strongly in its inspiration. And in due course the Jews came to feel that the Christians had stolen their scriptures, and so Aquila and Theodotion made fresh translations from the Hebrew for Jewish worship.

So this explains where the idea of divinely inspired and therefore authoritative books came from. The first Christians inherited it, like so much else, from Judaism. But what about the word "canon"? When we use the word we generally mean a collection of books. But that is not the main meaning of the Greek word *kanon*. It meant a measuring rod, a rule, before it came to mean a collection of books. This is very illuminating. From the beginning, the church accepted a norm of orthodox belief and proper behaviour. Before it became a list of books, canon was seen as "the rule of faith". This was originally a summary of Christian teaching, believed to go back to what the apostles themselves taught. And any system of doctrine or book that claimed to be Christian was assessed by this "canon". It was not until the time of Athanasius in the fourth century that the word came to be used to describe the list of books that comprised this rule of faith, the canon of holy Scripture.

If the earliest Christians accepted the authority and inspiration of the Old Testament, as they did, on what principle did they make any additions to that collection of holy books? The answer must be Jesus himself. The Gospels show

how his followers were gradually driven to the conviction that he was no mere man, no mere prophet, but the ultimate self-disclosure of the one true God. The New Testament epistles, most of which were written before the Gospels, show how that belief dominated and energised the first Christians. God had spoken in the Old Testament Scriptures: but his final Word was Jesus Christ.

You find this very clearly stated by the apostle Paul, writing in the early 60s. In Colossians 1:15ff. he maintains that Jesus is "the image of the God we cannot see", the one "by whom all things were made"; indeed "all things were created for him." As if that is not enough, Paul has so clear a grasp of the cosmic significance of Jesus that he adds, "in him all things hang together." He is the principle of coherence in the universe – and Paul goes on to acclaim this Jesus as "the head of the Christian body, the church". This is no anticlimax. He is asserting that the Christ whom Christians worship is the source, sustainer and goal of the entire cosmos! He summarises his contention very tersely in Colossians 2:9: "In him the whole fulness of deity dwells bodily."

Earlier still, in his letter to the Philippians, written in the 50s of the first century, Paul had commended "Christ Jesus,

> who, though he was in the form of God, did not count equality with God a thing to be grasped, but emptied himself, taking the form of a servant, being born in the likeness of men. And being found in human form, he humbled himself and became obedient unto death, even death on a cross. Therefore God has highly exalted him and bestowed on him the name which is above every name, that at the name of Jesus every knee should bow, in heaven and on earth and under the earth, and every tongue confess that Jesus Christ is Lord, to the glory of God the Father. (Philippians 2:5ff.)

Just think of the implications of these words. They mean that Jesus had always been one with God; that he voluntarily laid aside those aspects of his deity that would have been incompatible with sharing our human condition; that he became one of us and died on a cross; and that God exalted him by the resurrection to the highest place in the universe and has bestowed upon him for all to see the sacred name of God. For it is to the divine love and judgment brought to us in Jesus that one day every knee will bow. A mind-boggling claim. But that is what the very earliest Christians believed. For these words of Paul can easily be translated back into Aramaic, the language of the first believers. The original Aramaic-speaking church believed Jesus to be divine, and for-mulated that belief into a hymn or confessional statement years before Paul translated it into Greek for the benefit of his Philippian readers! These passages, among many in Paul's writings, are particularly important because he wrote them within 20 or 30 years of the death of Jesus. He puts us in close touch with the beliefs of the first Christians.

But the really impressive thing is the way in which Paul's conviction that Jesus is divine can be found wherever you turn in the New Testament. There is no substantial difference between the various writers despite the fact that they wrote independently of one another, and in different parts of the Empire. They are all convinced of the deity of Jesus, just as they are of his humanity.

Each of the Gospel writers makes the point in his own way. Mark, the earliest, heads his work "The beginning of the gospel of Jesus Christ, the Son of God". Matthew is at pains to draw attention in his very first chapter to the significance of Jesus' name which means "God is Saviour" (Matthew 1:21) and to the fact that his coming into the world signified "Emmanuel" ("God is with us" [1:23]). Luke introduces Jesus with these words: "He will be great, and will be called the Son of the Most High; and the Lord God will give him the throne of his father David, and he will reign over the house of Jacob for ever; and of his kingdom there will be no end ... The Holy Spirit will come upon you," so runs the message to Mary, his mother, "and the power of the Most High will overshadow you; therefore the child to be born will be called holy, the Son of God" (Luke 1:32–35). John is the most explicit of all the evangelists, from his opening statement about the Word (his philosophical name for Jesus) being God, and that Word becoming flesh for us (John 1:1,14) to the end of the book where Thomas falls down at his feet and cries, "My Lord and my God!" (John 20:28). And in his penultimate chapter the evangelist tells us that he has deliberately selected incidents from the life of Jesus that will lead his readers to "believe that Jesus is the Christ, the Son of God" (John 20:31). John the evangelist believed it. He longed for others to believe it too.

The writer to the Hebrews begins his letter with this powerful testimony to the deity of Jesus: "In many and various ways God spoke of old to our fathers by the prophets; but in these last days he has spoken to us by a Son." And notice who this Son is. God has appointed him as "the heir of all things, through whom also he created the world. He reflects the glory of God and bears the very stamp of his nature, upholding the universe by his word of power." This divine, cosmic Christ "when he had made purification for sins, sat down on the right hand of the Majesty on High" (Hebrews 1:1–3).

This strong New Testament conviction that Jesus had brought God to our world carried the obvious implication that he was supremely authoritative. There is a remarkable claim found in identical form in Matthew 11:25ff. and Luke 10:21ff. where Jesus claims an exclusive relationship with the

Father. He alone fully knows the Father. He alone can introduce men to the Father. To him alone has the Father delivered all things. Let men and women therefore come to him. "All things have been delivered to me by my Father; and no one knows the Son except the Father, and no one knows the Father except the Son and anyone to whom the Son chooses to reveal him. Come to me, all who labour and are heavy laden, and I will give you rest." What religious leader ever spoke like that? He can do so with both humility and authority because he does in fact constitute the meeting point of God and man.

That supreme authority comes out with irresistible clarity throughout the ministry of Jesus. "He taught them as one who had authority, and not as the scribes," observes the evangelist Mark at the start of the ministry, and, as Jesus expels dark spirits from spoiled lives, the onlookers question one another, "What is this? A new teaching! With authority he commands even the unclean spirits, and they obey him" (Mark 1:22, 27). That double authority, in kingdom acts of power and kingdom teaching, continues throughout the ministry of Jesus. The unique "Amen, Amen I tell you", the parables, the debates with the Pharisees, the healings and the nature miracles all point in the same direction. Here is one who has God's delegated authority. No wonder that he claims in the Sermon on the Mount, "Think not that I have come to abolish the law or the prophets; I have come not to abolish them but to fulfil them" (Matthew 5:17). No wonder that Moses representing the Law, and Elijah representing the prophets, appear on the Mount of Transfiguration with Jesus, and enjoin on the astonished disciples, "Hear him." No wonder that in the great prayer before his death he cries, "Father, the hour has come; glorify your Son so that the Son may glorify you, since you have given him authority over all people, to give eternal life to all whom you have given him" (John 17:2). No wonder that, after his resurrection, as he prepares to leave his disciples and commits the task of world mission to them, he says, "All authority in heaven and on earth has been given to me. Go therefore ... and remember, I am with you always, to the end of the age" (Matthew 28:18–20).

Such, then, is Jesus, the Messiah. His influence, his teachings, his claims, his miracles, his fulfilment of prophecy, his death and his resurrection all combine to convince the first disciples that their Master is no mere man but Lord and God. They have heard the authority of his teaching and seen the authority of his miracles and supremely of his death and resurrection. Of course, then, they put his teaching at least on a level with the Old Testament. All Jews believed that God had spoken in the sacred Scriptures. That was common ground between them. But these Jews were convinced that the God who had inspired the ancient Scriptures had actually come among his people in the person of Jesus Christ. His words, accordingly, must be just as sacred as those ancient books of revelation: his authority must be as great. Accordingly, "It is written", or "Scripture says", the natural way for them to allude to the authority of the Old Testament, begins even in the New Testament writings themselves to be ascribed to the words of Jesus himself. In Paul's first letter to Timothy we read "The scripture says, 'You shall not muzzle an ox while it is treading out the grain', and 'The labourer deserves his wages'" (1 Timothy 5:18). The first part of the quotation comes from Deuteronomy 25:4 and the second comes from Jesus himself, as recorded in Luke 10:7. It would probably be going too far to say that this is the first example of the New Testament being cited as Scripture, but it is certain that this passage puts the words of Jesus and the words of the Old Testament on the same level of inspiration and authority.

Where did the church get the idea of authoritative, inspired books? It came from the Old Testament, which all Jews revered in this way. So the first Christians already inherited a canon of Scripture, even if, as is just possible, two books, Esther and the Song of Solomon, may not have had a secure place in it until the Council of Jamnia. The Old Testament was emphatically the Bible for these "people of the book". But they could not leave it there. The towering influence and authority of the God who not only inspired from afar but came near in human flesh meant that they had to accord him and his words a veneration at least equal to that which they gave to the Old Testament. The idea of a canon of Scripture all began with the Old Testament and Jesus.

Chapter Three

The New Testament Manuscripts - Can We Trust Them?

It is all very well recognising the conviction of the New Testament writers that Jesus shared the very nature of God, but the question arises very sharply of whether or not we can trust the record about him that we have printed in our modern Bibles. Does it go back to the original era? Or were the Communists right in supposing that it all arose from a revolt of the proletariat at the end of the second century? Or is Brown right that our Gospels were brought to prominence only in the fourth century by Constantine, and were much inferior to the earlier Gnostic gospels, which they replaced?

There is a famous and much-quoted passage about Jesus from the historian and moralist W.E.H. Lecky:

> The character of Jesus has not only been the highest pattern of virtue, but the strongest incentive to its practice, and has exerted so deep an influence, that it may truly be said that the simple record of three short years of active life has done more to regenerate and to soften mankind than all the disquisitions of the philosophers and than all the exhortations of the moralists.

His assessment is all the more impressive because he himself was not a Christian. Many people would agree with Lecky, but of course the character of Jesus can be known only from the

New Testament records. So it matters very much whether these can be relied on. A number of important questions suggest themselves.

What are the Gospels?

The Gospels represent an entirely new type of literature. They are not just biography – for they omit any account of many years of Jesus' life. Nor are they merely history, since they show comparatively little interest in the history of the Roman Empire in which they are set. Though they contain both biography and history, the Gospels are "gospel": good news. This was a rare word before the coming of Christianity, and was used first of the message the early Christians proclaimed, and later on it was applied to what they wrote. It was the good news of a living God who cared enough for his people to come and live among them, die for them, and rise again to newness of life, which he offered to share with them. Good news, in fact, of an entirely new chapter in world history. They were confident that the coming, dying and rising of Jesus was the most important event that had ever happened – and they wanted everyone to discover it for themselves. That accounts for the confidence and the the Easter faith that pervade all four Gospels. These writers passionately believed what they wrote. And their written accounts show us the way in which the first Christians went about preaching the good news of Jesus. Accordingly, the precise authorship of the different Gospels is comparatively unimportant. There was a living community of faith behind each author. And the authors themselves were in close touch with the immediate disciples of Jesus and their circle. It must be remembered that when the Gospels were written there were still plenty of people alive who had known Jesus and could check the veracity of any records about him.

Who wrote the Gospels and when?

The authorship and dating of the Gospels is a complicated matter which has exercised some of the best minds for over two hundred years. This is not the place to go into the intricacies of the debate, but the following summary would be widely accepted.

Mark's Gospel was probably written first, in the early 60s. He was a close companion of the apostles Peter and Paul. No doubt he drew on various sources, but the early and unanimous tradition from the end of the first century onwards is that he was the follower and interpreter of Peter, and took great care to present the gospel that Peter preached, and to make it widely available by consigning it to paper. Of course, Mark will have used other sources, but it is encouraging to know that his main informant was the man at the heart of it all: Simon Peter, the most famous of all Jesus' friends. Mark writes with a breathless urgency and enthusiasm, and almost every paragraph is about Jesus, mainly about what he said and did and how he met his death. It is very evidently preaching material put down on paper and has many vivid eyewitness touches, which Mark will have heard from Peter's impassioned addresses.

Within a few years Matthew's Gospel appeared. It was designed to meet the needs of the Jews who were flooding into Christianity, and to integrate them with the Greek members of the church. He was a very organised writer and addressed himself, I think, primarily to the teachers and leaders in the new Christian community of which he was a member. We do not know exactly who this "Matthew" was. The early Christians thought he was Matthew the tax-gatherer who became one of Jesus' disciples. But this is unlikely, both because he uses Mark's Gospel as his basic source and also because it would be very odd for an eyewitness to draw from the record of someone who was not himself present! Probably the name of Matthew became associated with this Gospel because it embodies a lot of special material that the apostle Matthew gathered. This was a collection of the many sayings of Jesus, absent from Mark, which also appear in Luke. Scholars call this the "Q" material, and it is clearly very ancient. Probably Matthew the apostle assembled "Q", the teachings of his master, Jesus, and quite possibly during his ministry. He certainly had ample opportunity to do this, as he followed Jesus for those three years. And as a tax-gatherer he must have had the writing skills and probably shorthand as well, which was well known in the ancient world. So once again we are brought back to bedrock, eyewitness testimony.

Luke wrote his Gospel at much the same time, possibly in the early 80s, though several scholars believe it was written some 20 years earlier. He was not a Jew, but a Gentile believer who was a close friend and associate of the apostle Paul and is mentioned several times in his letters. He wrote especially for the benefit of non-Jews who were becoming Christians. He was not one of the original disciples of Jesus, but he tells us at the outset of his two volume work (the Gospel and Acts) that he had carried out extensive research among those who had been eyewitnesses. It is obvious that Mark's Gospel and Matthew's "Sayings Source" were among the primary materials he examined and made good use of. The stories of the birth of Jesus and his early years were probably elicited from Jesus' mother, Mary, herself, as Luke spent extended time doing his research in Palestine (while Paul was imprisoned in Caesarea) before accompanying Paul to Rome. Luke met eyewitnesses of the resurrection, too, and included their material in his book. Luke has a particular gift for recounting the parables of Jesus: all the most vivid ones are to be found in his

Gospel. He also has a profound concern for the underprivileged, the women, the beggars, the outcasts, the poor. His greatest achievement is to see that the story of Jesus is only Part One of the continuing story of the church. His Acts of the Apostles is, as its opening verses assert, a deliberate continuation of the story of Jesus, and it is invaluable because it is the only account we possess of the first 30 years of the Christian movement.

The most majestic – and mysterious – of all the Gospels is that ascribed to John. He was the intimate friend of Jesus, with a strong mystical streak, and he brings a fresh perspective to the life and teaching of his Master. It is he, for example, who gives us the great debates with the Jewish leaders, and Jesus' profound statements about himself and his work. But although it is different, the picture John paints is undeniably the same Jesus that the others describe. It just seems as if John has got inside the mind of Jesus in a way nobody else did. The actual authorship of this wonderful Gospel has been endlessly debated. It now seems certain that it was written either by the apostle himself, or by a close associate at John's direction. Some people think that it was written before the fall of Jerusalem to the Romans in 70 AD, but most scholars agree with Christians of the second century in seeing it as the last of the Gospels to be written, in the 80s or early 90s, when the apostle was an old man, shepherding the church in the Roman province of Asia.

Such, in brief, are the Gospels. They were written between approximately 60 and 85 AD, that is to say between 30 and 55 years after the events they record. If we wonder why the writers waited so long, the answer seems to be twofold. On the one hand they hoped that Jesus would soon return to bring history to a conclusion. On the other, they were so busy spreading the gospel around the Mediterranean world that this took priority over writing books. It was only as the original disciples began to die off that the urgency of committing their message to paper became obvious. Curiously enough, all four Gospels are anonymous, though the early Christians, writing shortly afterwards, tell us who their authors were believed to be. This anonymity is not a weakness: it is rather a strength. These four Gospels reflect the joyful conviction of the whole Christian community that the Jesus who walked the hills of Galilee had conquered death, and was alive, calling people everywhere to come and follow him. The Gospels are, if you like, the tip of the iceberg, a tip that belongs to the great body of early believers hidden beneath the surface.

Can we trust what the Gospels say?

It is all very well to know that the Gospels originated within a few decades of the death of Jesus, but can we believe what they say? They make such amazing claims and tell such astounding stories about Jesus – can we believe them? That is, of course, the crunch question on which you must make up your own mind. But if their central thesis is true, and God did indeed come to share human life, you would expect some pretty amazing things, would you not? And there are very good reasons for trusting what the evangelists have to tell us.

In the first place, no books in the world have been subjected to such prolonged and detailed scrutiny as the four Gospels. Today their credibility stands as high as ever. They emerge from every test with their integrity unimpeached. That is a very good reason for taking with the utmost seriousness the accuracy of the picture of Jesus that they paint.

Secondly, what the Gospels tell us accords very well with the secular evidence to be found in Jewish and Roman sources. But of course it fills it out and puts flesh on it. What is more, it chimes in closely with what the apostle Paul tells us in his scattered references to the historical Jesus. Paul wrote in the 50s and early 60s, rather earlier than the first of the Gospels, and his allusions are all the more impressive because they are so casual. In his letters to the churches he had founded, he is not trying to inform them for the first time about Jesus: he is merely reminding them of what they had heard when they became Christians, some years earlier. It would be hard to find earlier or better supporting evidence for the trustworthiness of the Gospels.

Moreover, there is remarkable harmony in the picture of Jesus that the Gospels themselves present. He is obviously the same person, and his teaching and lifestyle are the same whichever Gospel you turn to. There is also an obvious accord between the message they embody and the pattern of the early preaching as we find it in Acts and in traces in other parts of the New Testament. There can be little doubt that such unplanned harmony between authors who were not colluding with one another gives us confidence in the report they give us. These Gospel writers were not making it up. They were telling us what happened.

A fourth factor is this. As mentioned above, many eye-witnesses survived into the 70s and 80s of the first century. If the Gospel writers were making up stories, or exaggerating them, there were still plenty of people around who could have pointed out their errors. And in that case the Gospels would not have gained universal circulation and credit. But apparently nobody could fault the Gospel records. We hear not a whisper of any such suggestion. They were known to be reliable. And so the Gospels became the bedrock of the church's teaching.

There are many other ways of checking the trustworthiness

of these remarkable little books. For example, had the church cooked up the contents of the Gospels, we should have expected them to have put into the mouth of Jesus statements about matters of burning concern to themselves. On the contrary, we find that these issues, such as the gifts of the Holy Spirit, the importance of circumcision and whether or not Christians could eat meat that had been offered to idols, are conspicuous by their absence in the Gospel record. That reinforces our confidence that the Gospel writers were recording things that were true, and not making up things that were convenient.

The parables provide another interesting insight into the reliability of the Gospels. People sometimes wonder if these parables go back to Jesus himself, or whether the early Christians made them up. But why should anyone pretend that Jesus taught in this remarkable way if he did not? Who could have been the genius to create them if not he? One thing is very clear. Although some rabbinic partial parallels exist, nobody before Jesus ever taught consistently in parables. Nor did anyone after him. It was his unique way of imparting truth. The early church did not teach in parables; but they knew, and faithfully recorded, that Jesus had done so.

Let us take two further examples which will help us to determine the trustworthiness of the Gospel record. One is what New Testament scholars call "the principle of multiple attestation". It simply means that there is added reason to accept the authenticity of some saying if it is recorded in more than one strand of the Gospel tradition. Well, let us apply that criterion to Jesus' feeding of the five thousand from a few bread rolls and sardines. It sounds highly improbable, does it not? Yet it is recorded in all four Gospels. You could not have better evidence than that.

The other tool is Aramaic. This was the language of

Palestine in Jesus' day. It is the language he usually spoke, though he was at least bilingual and probably multilingual. The Aramaic experts have discovered a remarkable thing. Much of the teaching of Jesus can be translated back into the underlying Aramaic. What is more, some of it falls into rhyming cadences. This is both beautiful and rare. But it would be a marvellous way to instil his teaching in a memorable way into a people who preferred the spoken word to books. No doubt Jesus taught in this way because he wanted his teaching to be remembered and accurately passed on. We have every reason to believe that it was.

I think the final fact that I find very persuasive is this: who could have made up the picture of Jesus that we get in the Gospels? It shows us a towering figure, different from any other who has ever lived – so sublime, so unexpected. Just suppose you and three friends were to sit down and write your impressions of the ideal human being. Would they not be very diverse? But the impressions of Jesus that these four evangelists record are remarkably harmonious. They are clearly portraits of the same person, revealing the same character, giving the same teaching, making the same claims. These men were writing fact, not fiction. They were trying to give an honest account of Jesus, and to nudge their readers towards becoming his disciples. Therein lies their unchanging power.

Can we trust the manuscript tradition?

This is a question often asked, and it is one to which we can give a very definite answer. We are in a better position to assess the reliability of the text of the New Testament than we are with any other ancient document. Take Thucydides, for example. He was the famous Greek historian who wrote the history of the Peloponnesian War, about 400 BC. The earliest manuscript of Thucydides we possess dates from the eleventh century AD. Yet no classical scholar of any stature has ever doubted that we have what Thucydides wrote simply because of the fourteen-hundred-years' time gap between his autograph edition and our earliest existing copy.

Or think of Tacitus, the distinguished Roman historian who wrote in the 90s of the first century. Books 1–6 of his *Annals* come from a single Latin manuscript of the ninth century. The second part of his work, Books 11–16, come from a single eleventh-century manuscript, and yet nobody doubts that this is what Tacitus wrote. It is only with Christianity, because the issues are so great, that people take refuge in questioning the reliability of the text tradition.

Now in striking contrast to this very slender manuscript attestation of these great authors such as Thucydides and Tacitus (and the situation is much the same with other classical writers, such as Julius Caesar, the earliest text of whose *Gallic War* dates from 900 years after his day), we have over 5,000 Greek manuscripts of the New Testament, the oldest of which go back to about 350 AD. In addition we have numerous papyrus codices or books, the oldest of which, P52, goes back to between 100 and 125 AD! This is a fragment of St John's Gospel, found in Egypt, and now a prized possession of the John Rylands Library in Manchester. The text is identical with the later manuscripts. The Chester Beatty Papyri, housed in Dublin and containing most of the New Testament, can be dated to shortly after 200 AD, while the Bodmer Papyri, housed in Geneva, contain much of the Gospels and Epistles and date from a little before 200 AD. There are no other ancient documents where the gap between the original writing and the first extant copies is as small as in the case of the New Testament. Moreover, the attestation comes in many languages from different parts of the ancient world, and this provides an immensely reliable text for the New Testament. Of course there are textual variants, but no single doctrine depends on a disputed reading, and the text of the New Testament is so sure that nobody dares to suggest conjectural emendations. We can confidently assert that we have the Gospels as they were written. There are only two serious questions. One is whether Mark 16:9–20 was written by the evangelist or added a little later to a Gospel that ended very abruptly at 16:8. The other is whether the story of the woman caught in adultery belongs in John 7:53 – 8:11, or after Luke 21:38.

Recent discoveries confirm the early dates of our manuscripts, and take us still further back. We now have a small fragment of Mark's Gospel chapter 6, found among the Dead Sea Scrolls, which were hidden in the caves by the Dead Sea when the Romans came to "settle the Jewish problem" in 66 AD. We have fragments of Matthew chapter 26 in Oxford which look on palaeographical grounds to have been written before 70 AD, though this is disputed. There is a document referred to as the "Unknown Gospel", written between 100 and 150 AD, which seems to draw from each of our four Gospels and thereby shows that they were all written and reckoned to be authoritative well before that time. The early heretic Valentinus, whose *Gospel of Truth*, written in Rome between 140 and 150 AD, has recently been discovered, quotes extensively from the New Testament writings that are in our Bible. So did the so-called "apostolic Fathers", the leaders of the generation following the days of the apostles. Thus the *Epistle* of Clement of Rome, *The Epistle of Barnabas* and the *Didache* or Teaching of the Twelve Apostles, all written around 100 AD, together with Ignatius (c. 107 AD) and Polycarp (c. 115 AD) are thoroughly familiar with the New Testament as we have it and quote it copiously.

So by 100 AD, if not a little earlier – that is to say, within the lifetime of some who had heard and known Jesus – the New Testament was not only written, but was on the way to being collected. Furthermore, from the outset it was regarded as authoritative – so authoritative that Christians quoted it with the same reverence with which they quoted the Old Testament. So authoritative that the heretics knew they had to quote it if they were going to win a hearing for their heresy. Accordingly, you find the late Sir Frederic Kenyon, a very distinguished authority on ancient manuscripts, summing the matter up as follows:

> The interval, then, between the dates of original composition and the earliest extant evidence becomes so small as to be in fact negligible, and the last foundation for any doubt that the Scriptures have come down to us substantially as they were written has now been removed. Both the authenticity and the general integrity of the New Testament may be regarded as finally established. (*The Bible and Archaeology*, 1940: p. 288ff.)

Chapter Four

The New Testament Canon - How Did It All Start?

It was important to make some initial assessment of the date, contents and reliability of the New Testament records before going on to pursue the topic that we began to examine in Chapter Two. How was the New Testament canon formed? This is a large question, and we shall need four chapters to examine it properly. But it is necessary to go into it in some detail, because of the claims that are currently being made for the Gnostic gospels.

Convinced as they were that Jesus shared God's nature as well as ours, it was inevitable that his followers should begin to accord his teachings no less importance than the Old Testament, which all Jews recognised as divinely inspired. A good question is whether Jesus himself envisaged any such extension of the Old Testament. But there is a prior question, which we must examine with some care. How did Jesus himself rate the Old Testament?

Jesus' view of the Old Testament

All the evidence points to the fact that Jesus shared the traditional Jewish view of the Old Testament as inspired by God. He believed that God himself stood behind the human authors of the Scriptures. This comes through strongly in all the Gospel material. Mark 12:36 is a good example. In an important discussion Jesus makes his point depend on the inspiration of the Scripture. "For David himself, *inspired by the Holy Spirit*, declared ... " and he goes on to quote Psalm 110:1. In Mark 7:13 Jesus declared that the Pharisees were making the word, not primarily of Moses but *of God*, ineffective by prioritising their tradition. When in debate with the Sadducees about the subject of resurrection (Mark 12:26), he says, "And as for the resurrection of the dead, have you not read what was said to you [not simply by Moses but] *by God*, saying ... " (quoting Exodus 3:6). Again, in an illuminating passage in John 5:36–47, particularly significant because the eternal destiny of the hearers is under discussion, Jesus refers to the Scriptures as the God-given witness to himself, of greater importance than either John the Baptist's testimony about him or the miracles that he himself performed. He says to the Pharisees, who were strong believers in the inspiration of Scripture, "You search the scriptures, because you think that in them you have eternal life; and it is they that bear witness to me; yet you refuse to come to me that you may have life." The Pharisees made Moses and his writings their hope; but Moses wrote prophetically of Jesus (verse 46). Moses' writings and Jesus himself both come from God. They are complementary parts of God's self-disclosure.

Perhaps the crowning example of Jesus' attitude to the Old Testament comes in Matthew 19:4, 5. It is all the more impressive because it is so natural. Jesus is quoting the words of Genesis 2:24, which constitute a comment passed by the author of Genesis, and yet Jesus ascribes the words to God himself. "Have you not read that *he who made them ... said* 'For this reason a man shall leave his father and be joined to his wife, and the two shall become one flesh?'" Clearly, Jesus regarded this statement of Genesis as deriving from God himself, even though the Genesis account does not directly attribute it to God. In a word, as Jesus put it, "the scripture cannot be broken" (John 10:35). A word of Scripture was a word of God.

Jesus himself is the supreme revelation of the Father, and the deepest levels of the Old Testament Scriptures pointed to him. On the memorable post-resurrection walk to Emmaus Jesus stressed that the Old Testament Scriptures pointed forward to himself and found their fulfilment in him: "And beginning with Moses and all the prophets, he interpreted to them in all the scriptures the things concerning himself" (Luke 24:27). And, as the writer to the Hebrews put it in his striking opening words, "In many and various ways God spoke of old to our fathers through the prophets, but in these last days he has spoken to us by a Son, whom he appointed the heir of all things, through whom also he created the world" (Hebrews 1:1ff.).

The apostolic role of interpreting Jesus

It is not surprising, therefore, in view of the shattering impact of Jesus on his followers, that they often failed during his lifetime to understand a good deal of his significance (e.g. Mark 8:17–21, 9:10; Luke 9:45). There was much that was obscure to them until the death and resurrection of Jesus shed a blazing light on his person and mission. But always in the past God had revealed himself both by his mighty deeds in history and by the record and interpretation of them in Scripture. Event and interpretation went hand in hand, and both were required – otherwise, revelation had not taken place. And so it would have seemed natural enough to his disciples when Jesus said to them, "I have yet many things to say to you, but you cannot bear them now. When the Spirit of truth comes, he will guide you into all the truth; for he will not speak on his own authority, but whatever he hears he will speak, and he will declare to you the things that are to come. He will glorify me, for he will take what is mine and declare it to you" (John 16:12ff.). A little earlier, in John 14:25–26, Jesus had declared, "These things I have spoken to you, while I am still with you. But the Counsellor, the Holy Spirit, whom the Father will send in my name, he will teach you all things and bring to your remembrance all that I have said to you." One of the functions of the Holy Spirit of Jesus who came to them at Pentecost was to bring crucial things about Jesus to their remembrance and to bear further testimony to Jesus in areas that they had failed to understand in the days of his flesh. The Holy Spirit would equip them to interpret the greatest event in the entire history of God's redemptive work – the person and significance of Jesus.

Jesus' authority entrusted to the apostles

It is important to notice that it was to *the apostles* that this important task was committed. They were to bear witness to Jesus, because they had been with him from the beginning, and they were to have the help of the Holy Spirit who would constantly bear witness to Jesus (John 15:26), remind them of what he had said (John 14:26) and guide them into further appreciation of Jesus, who embodies the truth of God (John 16:13). What we have in our New Testament, then, is the apostolic witness to the words and deeds of Jesus, and the meaning of his life, death and resurrection as the apostles were led to understand it by the Holy Spirit. That is why the apostles are sometimes called in the New Testament "the foundation of the church" (Ephesians 2:20; Revelation 21:14): they were in immediate contact with Jesus on earth. They are the divinely equipped interpreters of his person and achievement for future generations.

It will help us to understand the unique function of the apostles if we recall that they were commissioned messengers of Jesus himself. He called them, Mark tells us, so that they might both be with him and be sent forth to preach (Mark 3:14). To the Jew, the commissioned messenger, or *shaliach*, always carried the authority of his master – an authority, incidentally, which could not be delegated and pass to anyone else. "He that is sent is as he who sends him," said the rabbis. And this seems to be exactly what Jesus means in such verses as Matthew 10:40, "He who receives you receives me, and he who receives me receives him who sent me", and John 20:21, "As the Father has sent me, even so I send you." Jesus was sending his apostles out with full authority to represent himself. We see this happening during the ministry itself in a limited way, during the Mission of the Twelve. It is like a trailer of the main film that will follow later, with the Christian mission at large. In Matthew 10 Jesus sends out the twelve apostles, clothed with his authority (v. 1). Their message is his message (v. 7), to preach the approach of the kingdom of heaven. Their function is his function, as the prophets had foretold (Isaiah 35:5ff., 61:1) – to heal the sick, cleanse the lepers, raise the dead, and cast out demons (Matthew 10: 8). It is precisely the same function that he himself fulfils in the next chapter, where a message is sent to the disconsolate John the Baptist in prison that "the blind receive their sight, and the lame walk, lepers are cleansed, and the deaf hear, and the dead are raised up and the poor have the good news preached to them" (Matthew 11:5).

In other words, the apostles are so identified with Jesus and his work that they are uniquely able to continue it after his ascension, and to interpret it with authority to later generations – since "He that is sent is as he who sends him." They are the commissioned delegates of their ascended Lord, and as such their authority is his own. Thus in the great commission at the end of Matthew's Gospel Jesus can say "All power is committed to *me* in heaven and in earth. *Go* therefore, and make disciples ... " The apostles were clothed with the authority of Christ himself. Such was the purpose of Jesus.

Not only have we good reason to think that this was the plan of Jesus, but it was also the emphatic claim of the apostles themselves.

That authority claimed by the apostles

The apostle Peter, for one, had no hesitation in claiming that the same Holy Spirit who inspired the prophets of old was at work in the apostles of the Christian era (1 Peter 1:11, 12). And in his second letter he puts "the predictions of the holy prophets" and "the commandment of the Lord and Saviour through your apostles" on exactly the same level (2 Peter 3:2). Moreover, he includes St Paul's writings among "the other scriptures" (3:15, 16). Though at first sight this may look strange, it makes a lot of sense. For Peter had already maintained that what characterises Scripture is that men moved by the Holy Spirit spoke from God (2 Peter 1:21). If the same Holy Spirit was leading the apostles into all the truth, why should not their words and writings have the same authority as the Old Testament and the words of Jesus, whose mouthpieces they were (1 Peter 4:11)?

It was not only Peter who claimed for the apostolic teaching this position of equality with the authoritative writings of the Old Testament. The apostle John does precisely the same. This claim is present in 1 John 1:1–5, and is strongly emphasised in 2 John 10: "If anyone comes to you and does not bring this doctrine, do not receive him into the house or give him any greeting." Adherence to the teaching of the apostles is made the condition of Christian fellowship. Similarly in the Book of Revelation the same high claim is made, culminating in 22:18, 19, which claims finality for the apostolic message enshrined in the book. "I warn everyone who hears the words of the prophecy of this book: if anyone adds to them, God will add to him the plagues described in this book, and if anyone takes away from the words of the book of this prophecy, God will take away his share in the tree of life and in the holy city, which are described in this book."

The apostle Paul claims the same unique authority for the message of the apostles, whether written or oral. In Galatians 1:6–12 he invokes a solemn curse on anyone who departs from the gospel that he has been preaching and which he received from the Lord; for he knew himself to be an apostle of Jesus Christ, personally commissioned by the ascended Lord to be his chosen representative among the Gentiles. In 1 Thessalonians 2:13 he gives thanks that when the Thessalonians received the gospel message they "accepted it not as the word of men, but as what it really is, the word of God, which is at work in you believers". In his second letter to that church he says that rejection of his teaching carries the penalty of excommunication (2 Thessalonians 3:14, cf. 1 Timothy 6:3–5). In 1 Corinthians 2:16 he claims the very mind of Christ in his teaching, and insists that not only his doctrine but the very words in which it is couched are inspired by the Holy Spirit (1 Corinthians 2:13). In 1 Corinthians 7, where the casual reader might think he is at pains to distinguish between the authority of his teaching and that of Jesus, he exclaims, "This is my *rule* in all the churches" (7:17). He is the apostle of Jesus Christ, and therefore he has authority to make rules for the churches in his Master's name, even when, as in this case, he has no specific instruction from the historical Jesus to go on. That is why he can say, "If anyone thinks that he is a prophet or spiritual, he should acknowledge that what I am writing to you is the command of the Lord. If anyone does not recognise this, *he is not recognised*" (1 Corinthians 14:37ff.).

This is how the apostles viewed their authority in the church, and this is how they exercised it. In the Acts of the Apostles we find them building up the infant church, working miracles just as their Master had done (e.g. Acts 5:12; 13:9–12; 16:16–18) exercising strong discipline (Acts 5:1–11), issuing directives (Acts 16:4), organising the internal administration of the church (Acts 6:1–4) and preaching with God-given boldness and power (Acts 2:41–43). The fellowship and autho- rised teaching of the church is their fellowship and teaching (Acts 2:42). They are the Lord's representatives, both for the building-up of the church (2 Corinthians 10:8) and for judg- ing it (2 Corinthians 13:1, 2). An apostle in the name of Christ can even deliver a hardened and impenitent church member over to Satan (1 Corinthians 5:3–5), which presumably means exclusion from the Christian community. They were in every sense the Master's men, clothed with his authority, because they were chosen by him as his representatives, and their words carried his authority.

Their authority endorsed by the sub-apostolic church

This unique authority of the apostles to interpret Jesus was envisaged by the Master himself; it was emphatically claimed by the apostles. We must now ask if the early church which followed the apostles endorsed their claim. Did they regard the apostolic teaching as their standard in both belief and behaviour?

The answer is abundantly plain. They did. Not only is this clearly presupposed by the Gnostic appeal to esoteric apostolic tradition, which will concern us later in the book, but the orthodox Christian writers of the sub-apostolic age explicitly say so. The earliest of them, Clement of Rome, writing in about 95 AD, calls the apostles "the greatest and most righteous pillars of the church" and underlines their unique teaching authority in this very explicit passage:

> The apostles received the gospel for us from the Lord Jesus Christ who was sent forth from God. So then Christ is from God and the apostles are from Christ... Having therefore received a charge, and having been fully assured through the resurrection of our Lord Jesus Christ and with faith confirmed by the word of God with full assurance of the Holy Spirit, they went out with glad tidings that the kingdom of God is coming. So preaching everywhere in country and town, they appointed their first-fruits, when they had tested them by the Spirit, to be overseers and deacons of the future believers. (*1 Clement* 42)

In a later chapter (47) he invites the Corinthians to "take up the epistle of the blessed Paul the apostle. What did he first write to you in the beginning of the gospel?" This shows that Clement recognises the apostolic authority of Paul's writings to Corinth. In the same passage he is careful to distinguish the apostles Peter and Paul from Apollos, "a man approved in their sight". It is plain that a major church leader such as Clement acknowledges the supreme authority of the apostles of Jesus.

Ignatius of Antioch (c. 35–107 AD) was another major church leader at the start of the second century, and was the second or perhaps third Bishop of Antioch after the days of Peter's leadership in that city. We know nothing of his life, until, under a guard of Roman soldiers, he began an extensive journey towards martyrdom for his faith in Rome, probably in the Colosseum, where he would have been torn apart by wild animals. He was received en route with great honour by Bishop Polycarp in Smyrna, where he wrote several letters of encouragement to three local churches and one to Rome, begging them not to deprive him of the privilege of martyrdom! This remarkable man had an enormously high view of episcopacy – but he was very careful to distinguish it from the supreme authority under God that had been enjoyed by the apostles. He thinks the bishop is the very image of God, and yet he writes to the Romans "I do not command you, like Peter and Paul did. They were apostles" (Ignatius, *Romans* 4). It seems clear from a famous passage in his letter to the church in Philadelphia that he put the prophets, the apostles and the gospel on the same authoritative level. "I have found mercy, taking refuge in the gospel ... and in the apostles ... yes and we love the prophets too because they too pointed to the gospel in their preaching and set their hope on him and awaited him" (Ignatius, *Philadelphians* 5). He thus places the gospel (the story and teachings of Jesus, which constituted "good news" from God in both their oral and written form), the apostles (their oral and written teachings) and the prophets (probably shorthand for the canonical Scriptures of the Old Testament) on the same level. So we have Ignatius alluding, even at such an early date, to what became recognised as the threefold canonical authority of the Lord (or Gospel), the apostles, and the Old Testament.

Ignatius was certainly not alone in taking this view. Polycarp (c. 69–155 AD) was Bishop of Smyrna and a major figure in the early second century. As a boy he had known the apostle John, and because he lived to a great old age (he tells us that he had served Christ for 86 years) he is a very important link between the apostolic age and the great Christian writers such as Irenaeus who flourished in the middle of the second century. Like Ignatius, he was a man of enormous courage. Like him, he faced martyrdom for his faith, and was burned alive in 155 AD by the pagan governor in Smyrna when he refused to deny Christ. Much earlier, in 116 AD, he had written to the church at Philippi, "Let us then so serve Jesus with all reverence and fear, as he himself commanded us, as did the apostles who preached the gospel to us and the prophets who proclaimed beforehand the coming of the Lord" (Polycarp, *Philippians* 6). Again we see the triad of Jesus, and the *prophets* who looked forward to him, and the *apostles* who interpreted him. That was the core of the Christian teachings, and the early Christians were assiduous in guarding it. And Polycarp takes us right back to the apostolic age. Irenaeus (c. 130–200 AD) was a major author and bishop, with wide experience throughout the Roman world. He says of Polycarp: "He was not only instructed by apostles and conversed with many who had seen the Lord, but was appointed bishop by the apostles in Asia in the church in Smyrna. We also saw him in our childhood, for he lived for a long time and passed from life in extreme old age, a splendid and glorious martyr, after having always taught the things he had learned from the apostles ... proclaiming that he had received this one and sole truth from the apostles" (Irenaeus, *Against Heresies*, 3.3.4).

It is obvious how deeply rooted Polycarp was in the teaching of the apostles when you look at the amount he quotes them. According to J.B. Lightfoot, in this one surviving letter he quotes from 1 Peter eight times, Ephesians three times, 1 Corinthians four times, 2 Corinthians twice, Galatians four times, 1 Timothy three times, 2 Timothy twice, Romans twice, 1 John once, Philippians twice and 2

Thessalonians twice. So when he says "I am persuaded that you are well schooled in the sacred writings" and goes on to quote Ephesians 4:26, and in the same passage Galatians, 1 Timothy and Philippians, it seems beyond dispute that by "the sacred writings" he means the authoritative apostolic letters. Even as early as 116 AD, then, when Polycarp wrote to the Philippians, the authoritative teaching of the apostles of Christ was known to be mediated to the church through their writings. Perhaps this should not surprise us, since some 65 years earlier Paul wielded the power of an apostle of Jesus Christ whether by his presence or, when absent, by his letters (2 Corinthians 10:11). But it is a very important thing to bear in mind when we come to examine the position of later writings, often from very suspect sources, that were keen to claim the same authority.

These early Christian leaders were acutely aware of the distinction between the apostolic age and their own. They emphasised it both by minimising their own importance compared with the apostles of Jesus, and by quoting extensively from the writings of the New Testament. As time went on they freely applied the formula "It says" or "the Scripture says" to New Testament as well as to Old Testament writings. This is surprising only to those who do not take seriously the New Testament teaching about the unique function and authority of the apostles.

As a matter of fact, statistical word study of the Christian writings of the second century has come up with a fascinating discovery. Despite the fact that the Old Testament is nearly four times longer than the New, it is the New that is quoted a great deal more. Whether or not they were defined as Scripture, *graphe*, these books of the Gospels and Epistles had fast become the most important books in the world for believers, and it is these that they were keen to quote. There may be something, too, in the reflection that anything called "scripture" tends to be regarded as rather hoary and old, and these Christian evangelists were filled with joy in proclaiming the new thing that God had done in Christ. It was in sequence to the Old, to be sure, but infinitely eclipsed it. Indeed, so universal is this second-century reverence for the apostles and their teaching that the saying of Serapion, Bishop of Antioch in about 180 AD, "We accept the apostles as the Lord himself," could with no less truth have been uttered 80 years earlier.

Chapter Five

The New Testament Canon - How Did It Develop?

$\mathfrak{I}$f the apostles were pre-eminent in the formation of the canon, Paul was pre-eminent among the apostles. His conversion and personal call by God is written up in the New Testament more than any other event apart from the death and resurrection of Jesus. There are three major accounts in Acts (chs 9, 22, 26) one in Galatians (ch. 1), and another in Philippians (ch. 3), together with a further one in 1 Timothy (ch. 1). The singular impact of his conversion, his enormous intellectual and spiritual stature, and his unparalleled missionary activity in founding churches all over the Eastern Mediterranean, made him the outstanding person in the spread of first-century Christianity. And given the fact that he was highly literate, and so concerned for the development of the churches he had founded that he wrote pastoral letters to them on a variety of topics, it is hardly surprising that his writings occupy a large part of our New Testament.

The earliest New Testament writings

In broad terms, the letters of Paul are the earliest part of the New Testament to have been penned. That may be a slight exaggeration. The letter of James is believed by many scholars to date from the time when Jews and Christians were not yet differentiated. The church was still called "the synagogue" (James 2:2) and "the early and the latter rains" (James 5:7 – a very Jewish turn of phrase), "the Lord of hosts" (James 5:4) and the presbyters anointing the sick with oil (James 5:14) all seem to point to very early Palestinian Christianity. The vivid expectation of the Lord's return makes a late date improbable (James 5:1–9). Moreover, chapter two shows awareness of Paul's slogan of "justification by faith", but also shows that Paul's teaching on the subject was misunderstood. This would be hard to imagine if the letter is later than the Apostolic Council on the topic of Christian initiation held in 48 AD. Probably, then, the letter was written a little before that date.

Another very early part of the New Testament is what scholars call the Little Apocalypse, Mark 13, and parallel passages in Luke and Matthew. Jesus is interweaving two predictions, and issuing warnings on both. They are the destruction of Jerusalem (70 AD) and the end of all history. There is a passage about what action to take when a "desolating sacrilege" was "set up where it ought not to be – let the reader understand" (Mark 13:14). The allusion is obviously to the horrendous occasion when in 167 BC the conquering Syrian ruler, Antiochus Epiphanes, set up an altar to himself as "Zeus made manifest" in the most holy part of the Jewish Temple. It looked as if history would be repeated. For in 40 AD the Roman Emperor, Caligula, crazed with self-importance and claiming to be divine, ordered the governor of Syria to go and set his statue up in the same place. The governor realised this would be madness, and dragged his feet. Mercifully, Caligula was murdered before this could be carried out. But the fear that this appalling sacrilege would be committed was rife in the early Christian and Jewish communities, and it may well be the case that these words of Jesus were written down and given wide circulation (and mistaken application!) at this time.

It is very likely that the story of the passion of Jesus came to be written down very early, too. In however truncated a form it would have been told as the Christian community frequently gathered to do what Jesus had bidden them, to eat bread and drink wine in memory of his sacrifice for them. To begin with, the story would have been told orally, but the accounts in Matthew, Mark, Luke and 1 Corinthians 11 indicate that there is a written form of the institution of the Lord's Supper underlying them. That would point to a very early date.

The letters of Paul

But these are exceptions. By far the most significant body of early material in the New Testament comes from the hand of the apostle Paul. His earliest letter, to the Galatians, was probably written in 48 AD, white hot with anger that "another gospel" was being proclaimed which required the circumcision of Gentile believers. The matter was resolved at the Council of Jerusalem in the same year. His last letters were sent while he was in a Roman prison awaiting death, probably in 66 AD. So this body of letters covering 16 or 18 years, is, with the possible exceptions noted above, the earliest part of our New Testament. The Gospels were written a little later: for although the date of each of them is still vigorously discussed among New Testament experts, most would place them, as we saw in Chapter Three, between 60 and 85 AD.

Their collection as a corpus

The question arises, then, when were the letters of Paul recognised as authoritative? We cannot give a precise date with any confidence, but as we have seen in previous chapters it was early enough for men such as Clement, Ignatius, Polycarp and the authors of the *Epistle of Barnabas* and the *Didache*, the earliest of the so-called apostolic Fathers, to treat them with enormous respect, recognising that they had an authority qualitatively distinct from that of church leaders such as themselves. Of course the letters will have circulated separately to begin with, but from at least the early second century onwards they circulated as a collection. As early as the Chester Beatty Papyrus P45, written in about 200 AD, we actually possess the fourfold Gospels bound together in codex (book) form.

Paul had himself encouraged some circulation of his letters (Colossians 4:16), and there is evidence that both Romans and Ephesians were designed for a wider constituency. But the first reference to Paul's letters as a collection and as Scripture is found in the New Testament itself, in 2 Peter 3:16. So striking is this that many scholars see it as decisive proof that 2 Peter was not written by the apostle but by some forger in the second century. But this is gratuitous. There is no difficulty in supposing that Peter had read many of Paul's letters. The two of them were, according to Acts and Paul himself, in close and frequent contact, and they had Mark and Silvanus as common secretary–colleagues. As for putting Paul's letters on a level with "the other scriptures", is this such a difficulty? The apostles, as we have seen, were in no doubt that their written words were as authoritative as their spoken ones (1 Corinthians 5:9, 11; 1 Thessalonians 5:27; 2 Thessalonians 3:14). They had been commissioned by Jesus to interpret his person and carry on his work, and they were clear that the Holy Spirit who had inspired the prophets was active in and through themselves (1 Peter 1:11–13; 2 Peter 1:18–21). And that is why they required their letters to be read in church alongside the Old Testament (Colossians 4:16; Revelation 1:3; Philemon 2).

There is an ingenious suggestion that Luke may well have

been the first to gather together the letters of his friend Paul. His Acts would have provided the reader with no inkling that Paul wrote letters. But what if, after writing Acts, Luke (who must have known about Paul's letters although he had not written about them) began to visit the Pauline centres he had described, and to look for the letters there? As Professor C.F.D. Moule, who put this theory forward, points out, nobody knew better than Luke that the letters were written, and it is entirely in keeping with his temperament as a historian to collect them.

The influence of Marcion, Valentinus and Montanus

Be that as it may, we know that the Pauline corpus, as the collection of his letters was called, was published in about 140 AD. And it was a heretic who did so! His name was Marcion, the son of a bishop in Pontus (c. 100–160 AD). He was the archetypal non-conformist. He tried to get his views accepted in Asia Minor, but with no success. He then went to Rome, the centre of the Empire, and failed there too. So, like many after him, he formed his own church. He was a remarkable man. He built up an organisation that in less than a generation rivalled the orthodox church. It had the same episcopal organisation. It had the same sacraments. It had excellent organisation, and presented the ideal, attractive to many, of an ascetic life. He held a high view of the church, which he saw as the bride of Christ and the mother of Christians. Indeed, he claimed to be the proper successor of St Paul. As the historian Harnack put it, Marcion was "the only man in the early church who understood Paul – and even he misunderstood him!" Yet all the orthodox Christians of the second century agreed that he was a wolf in the Pauline fold.

Why?

The trouble was that he believed the "harsh" God of the Old Testament was quite different from the "loving" God of the New. He was determined to remove any suggestion of continuity between the God of the Jews and the God of the Christians. So he formed his own "canon". It scrapped the Old Testament and consisted simply of "The Gospel", which was an emasculated Gospel of Luke (the Gentile evangelist who had least to say about the Old Testament), and "The Apostle", which was a heavily edited collection of the ten epistles of Paul, omitting all quotations from the Old Testament, together with 1 and 2 Timothy and Titus, which would have been uncongenial – and were perhaps unknown – to him. He regarded the Twelve as hopelessly mistaken: they had corrupted Jesus' teaching with legalism. The only true apostle was Paul. Determined to allow no sniff of legalism and to reject any connection with the Old Testament, Marcion heavily edited both the Gospel of Luke and the Epistles of his beloved Paul.

Marcion was the first person known to us who published a fixed collection of what we would call New Testament books. However, it is very unlikely that he invented the concept of a canon of sacred books. Explicit definition is usually a function of exclusion, not of creativity. In any case, Tertullian, who wrote an attack on Marcion, accused him of excluding some of the sacred Scriptures of the church, and Marcion himself claims to have "purged" the epistles of Paul and the Gospel of Luke. That suggests that there was some sort of canon before him. If he did take the initiative in forming the first canon, in the sense of list of books recognised as uniquely inspired, it is hard to see why this heretic's collection was everywhere accepted within less than two decades. It is even harder to imagine how the Pastorals (as 1 Timothy, 2

Timothy and Titus are often known), Hebrews and a whole series of verses expressing the solidarity of the Old Testament and the New came to be inserted into his canon! It is much easier to suppose that he edited an existing corpus.

Tertullian (c. 160–220 AD) once said that there are two ways of wrecking the Scriptures. One was Marcion's way: he used a knife on Scripture to cut out what he did not like. The other was adopted by the heretic Valentinus. He used the whole *instrumentum* (by which Tertullian means the New Testament), but perverted its meaning by wilfully misinterpreting it.

Valentinus was a contemporary of Marcion who lived in Rome from about 135–160 AD. He was a leading early Gnostic, a sect whose views we will examine in a later chapter. But the interesting thing is that we now no longer have to rely on Tertullian's attacks, written with verve and spite some 60 years later. What is very possibly Valentinus' own work, *The Gospel of Truth*, has turned up in the sands of Egypt. It is one of the Nag Hammadi texts found in 1945, written in Coptic, which perhaps formed part of the library of a Gnostic monastery. It clearly presupposes and frequently refers to a large number of New Testament books, whose authority it assumes. The author knows almost the whole New Testament. Professor Van Unnik's verdict that "around 140–150 a collection of writings was known at Rome and accepted as authoritative which was virtually identical with our New Testament" (in *The Jung Codex*, ed. F.L. Cross, p. 124) may be a slight exaggeration, but it is not far from the truth. And the evidence from Valentinus' *Gospel of Truth* supports the view that Marcion did not invent the idea of an authoritative list of books: he was selecting from one that was already in existence. That accords precisely with the indications in the writings of Clement, Ignatius and Polycarp, which we have already noticed in the previous chapter. Thus it seems probable that there was a corpus of Pauline letters known and revered in both East and West before Marcion. Clement of Alexandria tells us that Valentinus made a distinction between the things written in "common books" and those found "written in the church of God" (*Stromateis* 6.6.52). This strongly suggests that Valentinus knew a canon of "church" books. Of course, the individual letters themselves were extensively read and revered half a century earlier. But maybe the errors of Marcion and Valentinus stimulated their collection and publication.

It is probable that the massive impact of Valentinus was another factor that urged the church to give sharper definition to the contents of its message. For Valentinus clearly knew nearly all the New Testament, but produced a totally new and speculative gospel, full of Gnostic ideas, tendentiously called *The Gospel of Truth*. It is not a gospel as we know it, but an amalgam of Oriental and Greek speculations, a little Christianity, and a lot of his own fertile imagination. It has almost nothing to say about the life and ministry and death of Jesus, but has to do with emanations from the Father, the birth of Error, the fall of Sophia, the "pleroma", and the secret knowledge that Jesus is supposed to bring.

It became abundantly clear that if the church needed to add to Marcion's list, it also needed some principle of exclusion to keep out works like those of Valentinus, which were promulgated with charm and flair, and gained a large following.

Moreover, there was a third force in the latter part of the second century which also had some considerable impact on the definition of the canon. This was the Montanists. Montanus, and his women colleagues Prisca and Maximilla, were three people with prophetic gifts who came from Phrygia, and they gave utterances in the name of the Paraclete (the Greek name for the Holy Spirit of God), claiming his direct inspiration. They were passionate Christians, ascetic in lifestyle, who insisted on the nearness of the end, when the Lord would return to this earth with his saints and rule for a thousand years. There was nothing particularly surprising about this. It was the accepted view of the last things during most of the second century. But local patriotism convinced them that the heavenly Jerusalem would descend in their own back yard, Phrygia. They insisted that the Holy Spirit was prophesying through them, and that those who did not accept this were guilty of sinning against the Holy Spirit. All this roused enormous interest, and split the church. After some vacillation the church at large rejected the Montanist claims to new revelation, and argued that the official church leadership were the ones entrusted with the teaching of the Holy Spirit, rather than charismatics with ecstatic utterances, whom the church had not authorised. In effect, the establishment of the day eliminated the Montanists by claiming that it was the priest who had the role of the prophet! This was a costly victory. On the one hand its identification of office and structure with spiritual giftedness tended to douse charismatic gifts, to the great loss of the church. On the other hand its refusal to recognise Montanist revelations reinforced the conviction that revelation had ended with the apostolic age, and helped to foster the creation of a closed canon of the New Testament.

The early Christians had not yet given sufficient thought to the limits of holy writ. However, the teachings of Marcion, Valentinus and Montanus forced them to turn their minds to it as a matter of urgency. Their response was vigorous, and can be found in all the orthodox writers from the middle of the second century onwards, men like Clement (c. 150–215 AD), Origen (c. 185–254 AD), Irenaeus (c. 130–200 AD) and Tertullian (c. 160–220 AD). They made plain that they accepted not one Gospel only but four (including the full text of Luke, which Marcion had mutilated, and named his *Gospel*). They accepted not ten letters of Paul as Marcion had done, but thirteen (thus including the Pastoral letters 1 Timothy, 2 Timothy and Titus). They accepted not only Paul's writings, as Marcion had done, but those of other apostles. They firmly rejected the unorthodox Gnostic gospel of Valentinus. And they accepted Luke's second volume, the Acts of the Apostles, which had not been much referred to before that but which, as they realised, was the critical link between the Gospels and the letters of the apostles.

That was a far-seeing and truly catholic response, in contrast to Valentinus' publication of a fabricated gospel and Marcion's sectarian concentration on only one apostle, and only one gospel account. Some in the early church tried to claim Peter, James, John or Paul as their special preserve. The Acts, and the catholic church subsequently, made room for all these apostles of Jesus Christ. Every genuinely apostolic testimony to the Word made flesh was to be accepted. What they excluded, as we shall see in later chapters, is material like that of Valentinus and a host of followers, who all came after the apostolic age. By then the waters had run too great a danger of getting muddied, or polluted by a dead sheep or two! They reaffirmed the instinctive intuition of the earliest sub-apostolic age, that they would draw water only from the upper reaches of the mountain, water that sprang from the apostolic source.

Why have written gospels – and why more than one?

The same generous, catholic spirit is revealed in the recognition of the fourfold gospel. To begin with, each of the Gospels had been the story of Jesus as recounted and cherished in one particular geographical area. But, perhaps because only four full-scale Gospels had emerged from the days of the first disciples, the catholic church gladly recognised them. This was so remarkable a conclusion that we need to look at it in rather more detail.

Why have written Gospels at all? The very early Christian Papias (c. 60–130 AD) used to say that he valued the spoken stories of Jesus more than anything written down. Both the Jewish and the Greek worlds rather looked down on written material, and relied on their long and accurate memories. However, as the first generation of believers began to die out, it became vital to preserve their message. The church fathers (as leaders before Constantine are called) tell us that Mark, the companion and "interpreter" of Peter, composed his gospel after Peter's death, to preserve the messages he preached about Jesus. Christians needed to know what Jesus had said. They required guidance on pastoral problems. They needed to inform ignorance and rebut heresy. Inevitably, therefore, written material began to emerge from the teachings of Jesus and the first disciples. Justin (c. 100–165 AD), a colourful Christian convert from pagan philosophy, calls them the "memoirs" of the apostles, and cites them more than a dozen times. He almost certainly means our four Gospels, and certainly everyone after about 140 AD means those four documents and those alone.

But why recognise more than one Gospel? This was quite a problem in the second century. In some circles only one Gospel was used. We have seen that this was the route Marcion took. Irenaeus tells us that in some Gnostic circles only Mark was used. In other circles they created a new one – hence the whole string of second- to fourth-century apocryphal gospels. Another way was to harmonise the gospel accounts into one narrative. There is an extremely early example of this in a very broken papyrus fragment from about the year 100 (known as the *Unknown Gospel*), which combines statements from all four Gospels with some very heterodox material. But there was soon a full-scale version in the *Diatessaron* (c. 160 AD), which conflated our four Gospels (and no others!) into one single account. This was written by Tatian, a Syrian Christian apologist and pupil of Justin. The massive popularity of his book in the church in the Eastern part of the Empire shows how acutely the problem of multiple gospels was felt. But all these attempts had one basic error, docetism. This is the name of an early heresy which refused to see both the human and divine natures of Jesus: truly divine, they thought, meant that he could not be truly human. He only seemed so (*dokein* in Greek means "seem"). It was the same attitude that was reluctant to accept the unity of divine revelation through the multiplicity of its traditions. The "catholic" (or mainline) church came to terms with the two natures in the one person of Jesus, and likewise with the unity of the gospel witness expressed in several accounts. The early Christians recognised that the Gospels were not so much biographies designed to convey information, as good news about Jesus, designed to produce faith and commitment. It seems likely that they accepted four Gospels for the very simple reason that these were the only ones that came from the apostolic age There were no others. Certainly we have no evidence of any. And this shows the enormously clear recognition of the principle of apostolicity by the second-century church. The apostles were the unique interpreters of the Lord himself. The church accepted what came from this source, and they were very suspicious of any other sources.

At all events, by the time of Irenaeus, c. 180 AD, the four Gospels were regarded as so certain and so unique as to be inevitable. There are four winds, says Irenaeus, four points of the compass, and naturally four Gospels (*Against Heresies* 3.11.8)! The Lord has given us the gospel in fourfold form, he says, but held together by one Spirit. And Irenaeus attacks any who reject the uniqueness of these four, and introduce either more or fewer faces of the gospel. This argument would convince nobody today: perhaps it did not then. But it shows how firm was the position of these four Gospels and these alone in the early church.

The Muratorian Canon

By the last half of the second century the situation is very plain. We have two lists of books that were recognised as apostolic in origin and authoritative for the church. They agree very closely.

The first is a list of New Testament books with some comments. Known as the Muratorian Canon because it was found and published by an Italian called Lodovico Muratori in 1740, it is substantial but incomplete, with many gaps and written in barbarous Latin. It seems to derive from about 160 AD because the unknown author refers to a book called *The Shepherd*, "written by Hermas in the city of Rome very recently, in our own times, when his brother Pius occupied the bishop's chair in the church of the city of Rome". The date for this is variously given as 127–142 and 142–157 AD. At all events it anchors the Muratorian Canon to a little after the middle of the second century. It appears to be a summary of the opinion of the Western church on the state of the canon at that time. It recognises the four Gospels, the Book of Acts and thirteen epistles of Paul, and then the document turns to books that are spurious or disputed. "There is said to be another letter in Paul's name to the Laodiceans, and another to the Alexandrians, both forged in accordance with

Marcion's heresy, and many others which cannot be received into the catholic church, *since it is not fitting that poison should be mixed with honey!*" This remarkable phrase shows the settled view prevailing in the church about the nature of heretical books. The Muratorian Canon goes on to list some of them: "None of the writings of Arsinous or Valentinus or Miltiades do we receive at all, together with Basilides and the Asian founder of the Cataphrygians (i.e. Montanus)."

And with that the fragment breaks off. It is a pity its text is not more reliable, because it is a very interesting list. It accepts our entire Pauline corpus, the two short letters of John (it had mentioned 1 John earlier), Jude and Revelation. It omits 1 and 2 Peter, probably accidentally lost through the omission of a line in the process of copying, since 1 Peter was never in doubt anywhere in the church. It also leaves out Hebrews. It was known and valued in the Roman church as early as Clement's day in c. 90 AD, as he quotes it a lot, but as apostolic origin was increasingly stressed if a book was to be accepted, Hebrews dropped out in the Western part of the Empire, since scholars realised it was not written by Paul. The omission of this fine and orthodox book shows how important apostolic origin was thought to be by the middle of the second century. For although it clearly came from the apostolic circle, it was not written by an apostle, and the Roman church knew as much!

It is plain that the Muratorian Canon makes no innovations (though strangely it includes the *Wisdom of Solomon*). It tells us what are the settled convictions of the Christians in Rome. And when there is a doubt, it expresses it. Thus it mentions an *Apocalypse of Peter* but says that, although it was orthodox, "some of our people will not have it read in church," presumably because it was fraudulently attributed to Peter. And the *Shepherd* of Hermas, also orthodox, was rejected because it was written "very recently, in our own times" and therefore could not come from the Hermas mentioned in the New Testament. As a second-century product it had no place in the canon of Scripture.

Irenaeus

The second witness from the last part of the second century is Irenaeus. He is particularly important because he knew the whole breadth of the Christian world. He was born and brought up in the province of Asia. Indeed, he was a pupil of the saintly Polycarp, Bishop of Smyrna, who was martyred in 155 AD, at the age of 86. And in his *Letter to Florinus* Irenaeus records his gratitude for what he had learned from Polycarp, including the old man's recollection of his contacts with "John and with the others who had seen the Lord". He spent some years in Rome and later emigrated to the Rhone valley in France, where he was elected Bishop of Lyons in 178 AD. Irenaeus was a leader and writer of great significance. Two of his works have survived, *Against Heresies* in five books, and the shorter *Demonstration of the Apostolic Preaching*. In Irenaeus we see the principal spokesman for catholic Christianity responding to Gnosticism and other second-century deviations. He did not leave us a list of New Testament books, unlike the Muratorian Canon. But he must have had one, because he quotes every New Testament book mentioned in the Muratorian Canon and also includes both letters of Peter, which, as we saw, have probably dropped out of the Muratorian Fragment. Quite likely Ireneaus knew the Muratorian Canon, since it is of Roman origin. Both of them draw attention to the list of books regarded as authoritative in the middle of the second century, and both of them in welcoming the honey reject the poison!

Of course there were further developments in the canon, before the final list exactly as we have it today was promulgated in the Festal Letter of Athanasius in 367 AD. But, as we have seen in the last two chapters, the broad outlines of the New Testament were crystal clear from the end of the first century onwards. The Gospels are so certain that their position is parallel to the four winds and the four points of the compass. The letters of Paul are so certain that they are cited by all the early Christian writers, Clement, Ignatius, Polycarp and Justin, while heretics like Valentinus and Marcion knew they had to use apostolic material if they were to have a hope of gaining a hearing for their heterodox opinions.

There were of course also regional difficulties in a pre-computer age. A little letter such as 3 John or 2 Peter had circulation difficulties and was not widely recognised. The Book of Revelation was accepted in the West but doubted in the East, perhaps because of its fierce allegorical language, while Hebrews was accepted in the East but doubted in the West (because they knew it was not Pauline). But by and large the New Testament canon was recognised early in the second century, and was firmly established before the time of the Muratorian Canon and Irenaeus in the middle of the century. "The Gospel, the apostles and the prophets" had been the threefold division of the sacred writings at least since the days of Ignatius at the very outset of the second century. They were seen as the norm for Christian belief and behaviour. And in someone like Irenaeus you have a direct line, through Polycarp and the apostle John, to the Lord himself. It makes for a very strong case.

Chapter Six

The New Testament Canon - How Was It Finalised?

We have seen an important process going on in the century after the apostles. Their supremacy as authoritative interpreters of Jesus Christ is recognised from the start, and instinctively put alongside the Scriptures of the Old Testament. Second-century churchmen saw the Old Testament as essentially a "Christian book" and yet they quoted the majority of books that we now have in our New Testament a great deal more often, particularly the Pauline letters and the four Gospels.

While that process of recognition and collation was taking place, two tendencies became obvious. There was a function of inclusion, as people came to recognise that certain books originated in the apostolic age; and one of exclusion, as unorthodox books were kept out. We do not yet have a closed canon, in the sense of an exclusive list of books. The edges of the collection are somewhat blurred. The *Shepherd* of Hermas, *1 Clement* and the *Didache* were all highly revered and in some circles regarded as authoritative. This was, I believe, because of the names of their authors. The books were orthodox in content and early, and the Hermas mentioned in the New Testament was wrongly taken to be the author of the *Shepherd*, while the Clement of New Testament days was equally wrongly regarded as the author of *1 Clement* (Romans

16:14; Philippians 4:3). As for the *Didache*, or "teaching of all the apostles", how could it be omitted if (as was wrongly thought) it carried the imprimatur of the whole apostolic band? So we see that the main core of books venerated and used as Scripture was solid and clear, but the edges were somewhat blurred and sub-apostolic books were rejected.

That process continued and was sharpened in the succeeding century. We find a progressive limiting of the books that could confidently be ascribed to the apostolic age and might therefore carry the cachet of apostolic authority.

Tertullian (c. 160–220 AD) lived in Carthage and was a powerful advocate for Christianity. He was the first of the Fathers to write in Latin, and though he remained a deeply committed Christian he joined the Montanists from about 206 AD. He was the first to designate the second part of the Bible as the New Testament. Clearly he had a collection of books that belonged in this New Testament, though he nowhere defines it precisely. But, as we have seen, he charged Valentinus with misinterpreting it and Marcion with mutilating it, so he must have had a pretty clear idea! It certainly contained the four Gospels and Acts, the letters of Paul, 1 Peter, 1 John, Jude and Revelation. He does not, in his surviving writings, mention 2 and 3 John, small letters with indifferent circulation. We do not know whether he knew them or not. But he was very keen on Hebrews, though it had not come down to him as a New Testament book; in his judgment it was worthy of being included among the apostolic writings. He argued that its author was none other than the apostle Barnabas, "who learned his doctrine from the apostles and taught it with the apostles". And as a rigorist he strongly approved of what he took (probably wrongly!) to be the teaching of Hebrews chapters 6 and 10 that there was no possibility of repentance after apostasy. But he had no patience with the *Shepherd*. Its moral teaching was not strict enough on adultery for his liking! We see two complementary principles at work here in Tertullian's assessment. One was apostolic authorship, the other orthodox content. These two principles continued to be decisive in the years that followed.

A parallel process of scrutiny was going on at much the same time in Alexandria, the centre of Christian education. Clement of Alexandria was a contemporary of Tertullian. In temperament, this gentle, civilised and highly educated man was very different from the fiery Tertullian. While Tertullian had fiercely rejected classical culture, Clement gave it a more positive evaluation and claimed all the best elements in it for Christ. His writings show an enormously broad knowledge of both classical and biblical literature. His surviving works show some 8,000 quotations, more than a third of which come from pagan sources, large numbers from the Scriptures of both Testaments, and a good few from heretical Christian writings.

The Gnostic movement was influential in Alexandria, and Clement had some sympathies with it. He saw the true Christian tradition as consisting in the "knowledge" which Jesus handed on to his disciples and they to their descendants. But he was orthodox in his beliefs and, instead of following the novel views of Valentinus, Basilides and the other Gnostic heretics, Clement regarded the Scriptures as the repository of our mature knowledge of God. He speaks of the two parts of the Bible as the Old and New Testaments, like Tertullian, but, like him, does not anywhere define a precise list of biblical books. It was still the age of testing rather than defining. He is clear that the law, the prophets and the gospel form a united authority for believers. The fourfold Gospel was a part of the tradition he had inherited, and he has some interesting things to say about the particular authors. But although the position of the four is incontrovertible, Clement may occasionally quote other writings such as *The Gospel according to the Egyptians*. This is a Gnostic work, which certainly did not come from the apostolic circle, but Clement can take a Gnostic saying in it ascribed to Jesus and reinterpret it in an orthodox and ethical direction without batting an eyelid!

As for other New Testament books, he revels in Acts, which he knows to have been written by Luke. He makes constant use of the Pauline letters including the Pastorals and, following Alexandrian tradition, of Hebrews. The Book of Revelation, doubted in some quarters, causes him no hesitations. We are told that in his lost book, *Outlines*, he wrote brief comments on every book in the New Testament, including all the catholic epistles – and, guess what? The "letter of the apostle Barnabas" and the *Apocalypse of Peter*. Moreover, he quotes other books that were circulating in the hands of early Christians but did not win firm recognition, such as the *Shepherd* of Hermas, the *Didache* and the *Gospel According to the Hebrews*. Beguiled by the name, several of the early Fathers thought the *Gospel According to the Hebrews* might have been an early forerunner of our Gospels, particularly Matthew – which was not the case. These men did not have our critical tools, though they were pretty shrewd. And Clement, with his cultured and literary background, was unwilling to reject good sayings or improving sentiments coming from books that were by any standard marginal to the Christian community. He is broader and more hospitable than Tertullian, but they both acknowledge the same core of authoritative and inspired Christian books that go to make up our New Testament.

Clement's successor in what was in effect the Christian University at Alexandria was Origen (185–254 AD). He was a giant of a man, and had the same breadth of mind as Clement, who seems to have been his teacher. His recognition of the New Testament books was the same as Clement's, but he began a distinction that became very important later on. He distinguished between the acknowledged or undisputed books, and those that were doubtful or disputed. In the former category we find the four Gospels and Acts, the letters of Paul, 1 Peter, 1 John and Revelation. He included Hebrews in the Pauline letters, as was customary in Alexandria, but he noted that the style of the letter differed markedly from that of Paul and concluded "who actually wrote the letter God only knows!"

The disputed books included Hebrews (in some circles, as Origen conceded), 2 Peter, 2 and 3 John, James and Jude. He himself is clear on the authenticity and apostolicity of all of these, but realises that their brevity or poor circulation prevented there being a consensus on the matter. But, not surprisingly for a follower of Clement, we find Origen including in the disputed category the *Letter of Barnabas*, the *Didache*, the *Gospel According to the Hebrews* and two he was very dubious about (with good reason!) the *Acts of Paul* and the *Preaching of Peter* ("it was not composed by Peter or by any other person inspired by the Spirit of God"). It was only the names of Peter and Paul attached to these documents that gave them any credibility at all. Those two names spawned a large collection of bogus writings in the second and third centuries!

Origen also has a third category for us, books that he calls "false", both because they falsely claimed apostolic origin and because their teaching was false. These included the *Gospel According to the Egyptians*, the *Gospel According to Basilides*, the *Gospel of the Twelve* and other assorted bastard works. One of the very interesting things about Origen is his strong doctrine of divine inspiration in the Scriptures, alongside his equally strong critical discernment.

This brings us to Eusebius of Caesarea, the first major historian of the church after Luke. He was born in 260 AD and was Bishop of Caesarea from 314–339. He sets out to trace the story of the Christian movement from the days of Jesus to the time of Constantine, when Christianity became the religion of the Roman Empire. He was a serious researcher, and were it not for him we would have no citations of early second-century authorities such as Papias. And where his sources have survived independently, they show that Eusebius was very accurate in his quotations, which gives us confidence when he cannot be cross-checked.

We can be grateful to Eusebius for clarifying the division that had been increasingly evident during the previous half-century. He divided up the books of the New Testament into three categories, the universally acknowledged books (*homologoumena*, he calls them), the disputed books, but recognised by most in the church (*antilegomena, gnorima d'oun tois pollois*), and the uncanonical books (*notha*).

Among the 22 universally acknowledged books were the four Gospels, Acts, the fourteen epistles of Paul (i.e. including the Pastorals and Hebrews), 1 Peter and 1 John. Moreover, he adds the Revelation of John "if it should seem right" as an acknowledged book (though he himself distrusted it because it was thought to teach a thousand-year reign of Christ on earth).

The disputed books, which are however acknowledged by most people in the churches, are the short letters of James, Jude, 2 Peter and 2 and 3 John.

As for the third category, the "spurious" books (meaning uncanonical), he includes the *Acts of Paul*, the *Apocalypse of Peter*, the *Shepherd* of Hermas, the *Epistle of Barnabas*, the *Didache* or *Teachings of the Apostles*, and with some hesitation the *Gospel According to the Hebrews*, acknowledging that "those Hebrews who have accepted Christ take especial pleasure in it." He adds, somewhat inconsistently, the *Apocalypse of John*, with the prefix "should it seem right. For, as I said, some reject it, while others count it among the acknowledged books." Does this vaccillation over Revelation mean that Eusebius did not know his own mind, or perhaps that he was coy about putting forward too bluntly a view that he knew most people, including the Emperor Constantine, strongly disagreed with? It is a fascinating discussion. Read all about it in his *Ecclesiastical History* 3.3.1ff, and in 3.25.1–7.

In Eusebius we have a critical mind coming up with much the same collection of the New Testament books that we have today, while showing uncertainty about the Book of Revelation, which was accepted in the West and doubted the East, together with the small letters of 2 Peter, James, Jude and 2 and 3 John. But note the way he had come to reject the *Didache* and the *Shepherd*, though previous generations had flirted with them. He had come to the conclusion that they did not derive from the apostolic age and therefore did not have a normative function for the subsequent church.

Thus far, apart from his rather ambiguous attitude to the Apocalypse, Eusebius' threefold classification is plain enough. But he appears to waver, suggesting that his category of "spurious" books might be rated with the "disputed ones" because they were known and valued by certain sections of the church. Though not canonical, they were at least orthodox in teaching. The same could not be said for other writings he knew, which falsely claimed apostolic origin but in fact promoted heresy. They are not to be reckoned even among 'spurious' books, but must be shunned as altogether wrong and impious" (*Ecclesastical History*, 3.25.7). A very firm repudiation of the Gnostic material!

Eusebius seems to have had a decisive influence on the canon. The Emperor Constantine asked Eusebius to let him have 50 copies of the Scriptures, both Old and New Testaments, in Greek. These were carefully transcribed by trained scribes, sumptuously bound and delivered in 337 AD. It is fascinating to recall that these same Christian Scriptures had been assiduously sought out and destroyed by the edict of Galerius, the last of the persecuting emperors, a mere 25 years earlier! This last gasp of dying paganism was most vicious in the East, as Eusebius knew well: he too had been thrown into prison. At all events we can be confident of the contents of Eusebius' Bibles. They contained the Old Testament as we know it, and the same 27 books that are in our New Testament today. Despite his own doubts, Eusebius must have included the Book of Revelation, because not only was it recognised by the vast majority of the Christian church, but it was a favourite book of the Emperor and he would immediately have noticed if it had been omitted. So, although we do not have a record of the complete list of the New Testament exactly as we have it until 367, there can be little doubt that the canon was firmly fixed by the time of Eusebius, more than quarter of a century earlier.

What we have seen in Eusebius and the two centuries that led up to it puts us in the position of being able to give a definitive answer to scholars such as Pagels and King, mentioned in Chapter One, who argue that there was no very clear distinction between orthodoxy and heresy until the time of Nicaea in 325 AD. Eusebius' carefully researched work, based on many scholars and witnesses before him, makes their position quite untenable. Even more untenable is the ridiculous claim of Dan Brown in *The Da Vinci Code* that "Constantine commissioned and financed a new Bible which omitted those (i.e. the Gnostic) gospels that spoke of Christ's human traits and embellished those gospels that made him godlike. The earlier gospels were outlawed, gathered up, and burned." Leaving aside the fact that the Gnostic material makes Jesus *much less*, not more, human than the four Gospels, the truth of the matter is that after the Emperor Constantine built his new city, Constantinople, he wrote and asked Eusebius, the most distinguished historian and Bible scholar of the day, to prepare 50 copies of the Christian Scriptures in Greek for the churches of that city. What Eusebius sent was not only identical with our present Bible, but represented the solid witness of the previous 150 years as to what books should be included! And none of the Gnostic material, so dear to Dan Brown, was ever considered for inclusion in the Christian Scriptures.

Finally, we turn to the letter of Athanasius, Bishop of Alexandria. In 367 he wrote a letter about the date of Easter, but the larger part of it concerned the canon and its limits. After his day the matter was recognised as settled. Athanasius was the first of the church Fathers who listed precisely the 27 books that we have in our New Testament, without making any distinction in their status. He adds these words:

> There are other books outside these, which are not indeed included in the canon, but have been appointed from the time of the fathers to be read to those who are recent converts to our company and wish to be instructed in the word of true religion. These are the so-called *Teaching of the Apostles* and the *Shepherd*. But while the former are included in the canon (i.e. the 27 books) and the latter (i.e. the *Didache* and the *Shepherd*) are read, no mention is to be made of the apocryphal works. They are the invention of heretics, who write according to their own will, and gratuitously assign and add to them dates, so that offering them as ancient writings, they may have an excuse for leading the simple astray.

For the record, Athanasius' list was confirmed by the Councils of Laodicea (363 AD) and Carthage (397 AD) and thereafter was, broadly speaking, secure.

So there we have it. After an exhaustive process of checking and rechecking, the church had come up with a list of 27 books that derived from the apostolic age and constituted the canon or measuring rod of Christian teaching.

The many heretical imitations were rejected with scorn. And the *Didache* and *Shepherd* were welcome to be read among Christian people, for they were orthodox and edifying writings, but they did not satisfy the criteria of apostolic origin. They did not come from the first days of the Christian faith, and so they could not be relied on to define its content. Apart from their orthodox teaching these two books seem to have enjoyed a popularity among Christians from the mistaken idea that Hermas, the author of the *Shepherd*, was the man of that name mentioned in Romans 16:14 while the *Didache*, an ancient and orthodox document purporting to represent the teaching of all the apostles, obviously had an a priori claim to acceptance. But when careful scrutiny revealed that both of these documents, worthy as they were, came from a period after the age of the apostles, their claim to be included in the canon of Scripture died. The matter was settled, and those books that derived from the first origins of the Christian movement were alone declared to be the criteria of its teaching. This was, substantially, a confirmation of the instinct that the Christians had displayed some 200 years earlier, in the days of Justin and Tatian. Only the documents that sprang from the apostolic circle were worthy of a place in the Christian canon.

Chapter Seven

What Principles Led to Inclusion - and Rejection?

L et us briefly retrace our steps. We have seen in previous chapters something of the development of the whole idea of a canon of sacred books, from the Old Testament onwards. The words of Jesus, and the teachings of his immediate and authorised interpreters, the apostles, were very early and very naturally added to the ancient books of the Jewish faith from which Christianity sprang. So now it is time to take stock, and remind ourselves of the principles that were at work, sometimes explicitly and sometimes intuitively, during the three centuries that followed the life and death of Jesus.

Did the church impose a canon?

Perhaps the most surprising and interesting feature of the whole process is this. Nobody sat down and determined the extent of the canon in the first three centuries. No church directive or Council of Bishops defined its limits. In his 1962 book *The Problem of the New Testament Canon*, Kurt Aland, a distinguished New Testament scholar and editor of today's most widely used Greek New Testament, says this about the canon: "It was not imposed from the top, be it by bishops or synods, and then accepted by communities ... The organised church did not create the canon: it recognised the canon that had

81

been created." That is the truth. Believers seem instinctively to have recognised the greatness of their holy books which emerged from the first days of the Christian faith. This should not surprise us. It would not add to the authority of a Bach oratorio or a Beethoven symphony if all the music authorities in the world got together to declare the greatness of these compositions. We know that instinctively already. No authorisation by musical authorities could add to – or detract from – that conviction. In the same way the four Gospels and the writings of Paul, Peter and John had that ring of truth about them, and the churches instinctively recognised it.

This is particularly obvious when we come to Eusebius in the early fourth century. He was the first genuine church historian who took pains to research the origin of biblical books. Despite his access to the extensive Christian libraries at Jerusalem and Caesarea, it is clear that he has no definitive official list to go on. Although he amasses an enormous number of references to Scripture in previous generations, he can cite not a trace of any official declaration canonising Scripture. For the most part, the Christians seem intuitively to have known what was authentic and authoritative. So Eusebius, anxious for certainty, sets to work himself. He writes extensively on the topic in his *Church History* 3.25.1–7. As we saw in the preceding chapter, he offers three classifications. First there were those 22 writings to whose authority and authenticity all his past authorities bore unanimous witness (the *homologoumena*, as he calls them).

Second, he records five short books that were disputed but recognised by most people in the church.

His third category contains books that were not deemed canonical. They were spurious (*notha*). It is clear that by "spurious" Eusebius means little more than "broadly orthodox but uncanonical".

It is only when he turns to heretical writings that he adopts a very different tone. There is no trace of ambiguity when he speaks of the books that the church rejects and suppresses. His evaluation is worth repeating. Such books, he says, are "brought forward by heretics under the name of the apostles; they include gospels such as those of Peter, Thomas and Matthias, and some others as well, or Acts such as those of Andrew and John and other apostles. None of these has been deemed worthy of citation in the writings of any in the succession of churchmen. Indeed, the stamp of their phraseology differs widely from the apostolic style, and the opinion and policy of their contents are as dissonant as possible from true orthodoxy, showing clearly that these are the figments of heretics. Therefore they are not to be reckoned even among 'spurious' books but *must be set aside as altogether worthless and impious* (my italics)". This is how Eusebius, the greatest church historian since Luke, dismisses the books (such as the *Gospel of Philip* and the *Gospel of Mary*) that men like Dan Brown in *The Da Vinci Code* regard as more authentic than our four Gospels! And in so doing he is expressing and confirming the intuitive conviction of generations of Christians before him. The church did not impose some list of books for the faithful to regard as authoritative. They recognised one! The books were already there, a deposit from the apostolic age, and their testimony to Jesus had the ring of truth about them which was recognised by Christians as surely as a jeweller recognises gold.

But of course there were tests at work. We saw that in the New Testament documents themselves. When prophets claimed to speak in the name of the Lord, Paul required them to submit their message to being evaluated by others (1 Corinthians 14:29). A little later the apostle John suggests a specific test of authentic Christian teaching: "Every spirit which confesses that Jesus Christ is come in the flesh is of God" and therefore "if anyone comes to you and does not bring this doctrine, do not receive him into the house or give him any greeting; for he who greets him shares his wicked work" (1 John 4:2; 2 John 10). In this way, the very first Christians were taking pains specifically to exclude the beginnings of the Gnostic heresy that some modern theologians, playwrights and novelists are so keen to advocate.

The test of apostolic origin

Since Jesus himself had left nothing in writing, the most authoritative documents writings available to the Christian community were those which came from his immediate circle. We saw in Chapter Four that the principle of apostolicity was central to the idea of a canon, and that it stems from the earliest days of the Christian community – indeed from the lifetime of Jesus himself. He appointed the Twelve to be his apostles, his *shelichim*, a word with very special meaning in Judaism. It meant a representative equipped with the full powers of his principal. That Jesus saw the Twelve in this light has been abundantly demonstrated by Rengstorf's article on "apostle" in the Kittel *Wordbook of the New Testament*, and in the writings of men such as F.J.A. Hort, N. Geldenhuys, Newton Flew and Oscar Cullman. "He that is sent is as he who sends him," said the rabbis, and this is exactly what Jesus means by saying to the Twelve as they go out on mission, "Whosoever receives you receives me" (Matthew 10:40). Again, after his resurrection when they are about to go into the world, he says, "As the Father has sent me, even so I send you" (John 20:21). The apostle is the plenipotentiary representative of Jesus.

As we can see when the disciples were seeking a replacement for Judas, the qualifications for an apostle were to have been a follower of Jesus in the days of his public ministry, to be a witness to the resurrection, and to be someone specifically called by the Lord (Acts 1:22). The exception was Paul himself, who probably was not familiar with Jesus in the days of his flesh but was very definitely a witness to his risen life and specifically called by Christ for this role. It is interesting to note that the Jewish *shaliach* (apostle) could not hand on his commission to anyone else; it was for him alone. And that presumably is why the apostles did not appoint any further apostles after them, but presbyter-bishops instead. There was something unique and unrepeatable about their position. They were the guarantors of the continuity between the incarnate Jesus who walked the streets of Palestine and the glorified Jesus whom the church worshipped. You can only have one generation of eyewitnesses of the resurrection, only one bottom storey to a building. And that is how the New Testament sees them (Ephesians 2:20; 3:5; Revelation 21:14). They belong, in the striking words of Oscar Cullmann, "more to the age of the incarnation than to that of the church". In fact, so close is the identity between the Sender and the sent, the Lord and his apostle, that the New Testament can regard the apostolic tradition about Jesus as almost identical with the Lord himself. Thus Paul can say about the Last Supper, when repeating words he must have got from someone present (i.e. it was a tradition about Jesus), that he "received it from the Lord" (*para tou kuriou*, 1 Corinthians 11:23). He puts on the same level apostolic tradition like this and the Damascus road experience, where he uses exactly the same phrase ("I received from the Lord", Galatians 1:12), because in both of them the ascended Jesus is directly at work.

Similarly, in a remarkable passage in Colossians 2:6–8 Paul can identify the Lord with the apostolic tradition in the same breath as he castigates the "traditions of men". They have received the apostolic message about Jesus, and responded to the Jesus who is embodied within that tradition and controls it – whereas the "traditions of men" are firmly repudiated (verse 8). The tradition of the apostles is quite different from the traditions of men. Its author is the ascended Lord, its content the Lord himself, its agents the divinely authorised apostles of Jesus, eyewitnesses with access to first-hand information, and their message is safeguarded by the Lord the Spirit. The traditions of men, on the other hand, spring from men alone, and their content is many removes from first-hand information. Their agents are self-authorised teachers who have no knowledge of the incarnate Jesus and were not witnesses of his resurrection. So there is only one legitimate tradition in the church, authorised by the Lord, controlled by his Spirit, almost equated with him, because proclaimed by his authorised representatives and witnesses of the resurrection, the apostles. There is no tension between Scripture and authorised tradition in the church. They are the same thing!

As we saw in Chapter Four, not only did the apostles claim this authority as interpreters of Jesus, but the early Christians clearly accepted it, and made a clear distinction between the apostolic age, the age of revelation, and their own day. The earliest Fathers of the church were at one in regarding the apostles and their writings as in an entirely different category from themselves. They treated the apostles with very much the reverence that they accorded to the Lord himself. For they were the specially authorised representatives of Jesus.

Accordingly, the first Christians naturally accepted the genuine letters of Paul, Peter and John. There was extended hesitation about 2 Peter and 2 and 3 John, as we have seen, but that was largely because the letters were not widely circulated and time had to be taken to ensure that they were not falsely attributed to the apostles, as a good many other works were. After a period of lengthy examination they passed with flying colours. As for the Gospels, two of them, Matthew and John, came with an apostolic attribution. The other two were closely linked with apostles. You did not have to be an apostle in order to have your work recognised as apostolic: you needed to be in close touch with the apostolic circle and its teaching about Jesus. So we find that, as early as the witness of Papias, Mark is said to have set down in writing Peter's witness to the words and actions of Jesus. Similarly, Luke was the "beloved physician" (Colossians 4:14), the close companion of St Paul, and the one who wrote a two-volume account of the origins of the Christian movement. It was the apostles or "apostolic men" who were seen as the fountainhead of authentic Christian tradition.

This accounts for the remarkable up-and-down fortunes of the epistle to the Hebrews, which we have already had occasion to mention. Hebrews is very early, and was quoted extensively by Clement in his letter a few years before the end of the first century. It was also known to Hermas a few years later. But then it drops out of the picture in the West, possibly because it was known not to be Pauline. But it was valued in Alexandria, where it was reckoned by Pantaenus and Clement to have been written by Paul. But Origen, Clement's successor, disagreed: "The thoughts are Paul's but the diction and composition are those of a companion. If then any church hold this Epistle to be Paul's we cannot find fault with it for so doing, for it was not without reason that the men of old have handed it down as Paul's. But who wrote the Epistle, God knows!" This became the general line in Alexandria. The letter was Pauline, at least in content, though not penned by him. Tertullian in Carthage reckoned it was written by Barnabas. It was largely neglected from then on in the West until Athanasius, the Bishop of Alexandria and champion of orthodoxy, came to Rome and informed them that it was indeed Pauline. So we find Jerome and Augustine accepting it, with some hesitation: "I am moved by the prestige of the eastern churches!" said Augustine! It is ironic that Rome eventually accepts Hebrews for the wrong reason, because it was said to be Pauline. But they were right to do so, for although almost certainly not Pauline it undoubtedly comes from the apostolic circle (see Hebrews 13:23). And so it has every right to be accepted into the canon for the same reasons as Luke and Mark – and indeed Jude and James, for both of these short letters were believed, probably rightly, to come from the brothers of Jesus and so to share in the authority of the central core of the earliest church. In any case it is plain that if a document came from the apostolic circle it commanded the allegiance of the Christian community in a way no other document did.

The test of orthodoxy

A second test concerned orthodox content, and by that they meant conformity with apostolic teaching. This became very important in the second century when the church was faced by two innovations, the views of Valentinus and Marcion. Their opinions were, as we have seen, very different, but the church leaders knew that this was not what they had heard from the beginning (1 John 2:24). So the church developed a rule of faith, a summary of the tenets of the apostolic gospel. It is sometimes called "the rule of truth" or "the canon of truth", and the second-century writers such as Irenaeus, Clement of Alexandria, Dionysius of Corinth and Hippolytus were keen to insist that it is the truth itself that is the standard by which any teaching is to be judged. Writings that had any pretension to be authoritative had to be judged on the nature of their contents. As the Muratorian Canon strenuously insisted, it will not do to have "poison mixed with honey". From the earliest days of the second century, when Gnosticism first reared its head with men like Basilides, Christians would have none of it. A man called Agrippa Castor, whose work has now completely disappeared, launched what Eusebius called "a most powerful refutation of Basilides". And the same fierce refutation of all forms of Gnosticism followed for more than a hundred years, notably at the hands of Justin, Irenaeus and Tertullian. The contents of these Gnostic works simply did not match up to the original apostolic core of doctrine. They represented a faith entirely different from Christianity. They were to be suppressed. Among them, of course, are the documents so beloved by modern revisionists, the *Gospel of Mary* and the *Gospel of Philip*. You only have to glance at a page of these works to see what a farrago of theosophical nonsense they are: they are a world away from the writings of the New Testament.

Not only did the church make credal summaries of orthodox doctrine, which we see beginning as early as the "faithful sayings" of the Pastoral epistles and the insistence in the Johannine letters on the physical incarnation of Jesus, but Irenaeus in particular based some of his argument against heresy on an appeal to the churches that were known to have been founded by apostles. The Gnostics claimed that it was they who had preserved both the genuine teaching of the apostles and the more esoteric apostolic teaching delivered to selected disciples worthy enough to receive it. So Irenaeus went to work to examine such claims and establish the content of genuine apostolic tradition. He was able to show that this authentic apostolic tradition was maintained in living power in those churches that were founded by the apostles and where there had been a regular succession of bishops or elders since their foundation. A major function of the bishop was to safeguard the apostolic teaching. Of course, none of the heretical teachers could do anything comparable, because their teachings were novel. Further, Irenaeus likes to test their claims against the "rule of truth" in the Scriptures: "setting each word in its context and adjusting it to the body of truth", he "strips it of their fiction and shows their inconsistency" (*Against Heresies* 1.9.4).

The appeal to orthodoxy is very obvious, in Bishop Serapion's dealing with the village of Rhossus and their affection for a supposed *Gospel of Peter*. We shall examine it more closely on page 143. When he read the book, he saw that its account of Jesus' death was tinged with docetism, and forbade its use. It did not suffice to have an apostolic name. It must have an apostolic content if it was to be received by Christians throughout the world.

The test of catholicity

The third test that was applied to any documents that claimed an authoritative status was whether or not they had been known and used by Christians worldwide and for a long time. Catholicity had been defined in the fifth-century so-called Vincentian Canon as "what has been believed everywhere, always and by all", and that is the criterion that the church sought to bring to bear. Continuous acceptance by and proven usefulness to the church at large was an important consideration. A work that had received only local recognition was not likely to be acknowledged as part of the canon for the worldwide church. Books, however, that had long been recognised by the majority of the church over the years were very likely to receive universal recognition in the end – we see that happening with Hebrews, which was long doubted in the West, and Revelation, which was long doubted in the East.

Geographical considerations must have played a very important part in the recognition of sacred books. The Roman world was vast, there was no printing, and the circulation of documents was hazardous. Eusebius draws attention to this criterion when he expresses his doubts about 2 Peter because it had not been quoted by "the ancient presbyters". Its restricted attestation and the bad state of the text have led some scholars to suppose that for a time it may have existed in either very few copies or perhaps only a single one. If so, it would fully explain its poor recognition among the ancient presbyters!

Apostolicity, orthodoxy and catholicity – these were the main critical tools in the early church for the acceptance of a book as Scripture. So if anyone came along in the second or third century touting the claims of a book that nobody had ever heard of, it would not get into the canon. If it was deliberately pseudonymous, as most of the Gnostic material was, that ruled it out of court. If it was written after the apostolic age, that too would seal its fate. When you consider the limited critical tools available to the early Christians, it really is remarkable that the major parts of the New Testament – the four Gospels, the Pauline letters, 1 Peter and 1 John – had established themselves worldwide by the start of the second century and never looked back, while gradually the three principles we have glanced at above sorted out the wheat from the chaff and gave us the New Testament as we have it. It is not the uncertainties on the edge of the canon that should cause us surprise, but rather the early and universal acceptance of the major part of it, in the face of a lot of non-apostolic and heretical material that circulated in the second and third centuries. I believe we can justly conclude that this was due both to God's supervision and to the intuitive recognition among most Christians of the truth and inspiration of the materials emanating from the apostolic circle.

Chapter Eight

Who Were the Gnostics?

The Gnostics have been alluded to from time to time in the preceding chapters, and now it is high time to look into this strange but influential underworld. Who were these people, and why were they so troublesome to orthodox Christians?

Curiously enough, nobody really knows the origins of the Gnostic movement, though clearly it emerged from fringe Judaism and Christianity. There is learned debate as to whether Gnosticism predated Christianity and had pagan origins, but the fact of the matter is that no Gnostic document that we possess can be dated earlier than the rise of Christianity. It appeared as a movement within broadly Christian parameters, and was a perversion of the Christian faith in the direction of speculative theology. It is really weird stuff. Here is an example, recorded in Irenaeus *Against Heresies* 1.14.1:

> This Mark (a Valentinian magician), who says that as the Only Son he was the womb and receptacle of the Silence of Colorbasus, sent into the world the seed deposited in him. The Tetrad from the highest invisible ineffable places came down to him in feminine form since, he said, the world could not endure the masculine element she possesses, and she showed him who she was and told him alone the genesis of everything, which she had not revealed to gods or men.

Or try this, from chapter 1.29.2:

Afterwards from Thought and Logos was emitted Self-Born as a representation of the great Light; it was greatly honoured and all things were subjected to it. With it was emitted Truth, and thus there was another pair, Self-Born and Truth. From the Light which is Christ and from Imperishability four luminaries were emitted to stand about Self-Born; again, from Will and Eternal Life four emissions took place to serve the four luminaries. These emissions were called Grace, Willing, Intelligence, and Thinking. Grace was united with the first great Light, Saviour, also called Armozel; Willing with the second, called Raguel; Intelligence with the third, called David; Thinking with the fourth, called Eleleth.

How about this for fantastic language and ludicrous content? You will find it in chapter 1.11.3:

There exists before everything a pre-unintelligible Pre-principle which I call Unicity. With this Unicity there coexists a Power which I call Unity. This Unity and this Unicity, being one, emitted without emitting a Beginning of all things, intelligible, unengendered and invisible, the Beginning which language calls Monad. With this Monad there coexists a Power of the same substance, which I call One. These Powers, Unicity, Unity, Monad and One, emitted the rest of the Aeons.

Not only is much of the Gnostic material sheer rubbish, but it is clearly incompatible with the teaching of the church. Consider this example from the *Gospel of Philip*:

Some said Mary conceived by the Holy Spirit. They are wrong. They do not know what they are talking about. When did a woman ever conceive by a woman? Mary is the virgin whom no power defiled. She is a great anathema to the Hebrews who are the apostles and apostolic men. This virgin whom no power defiled [...] the powers defile themselves. And the lord [would] not have said "My [father who is in heaven] unless he had another father, but he would simply have said ['My father']".

Now that is slightly more coherent, despite the lacunae, or gaps in the text, but see how different it is from the New Testament (on whose Lord's Prayer it is clearly dependent). First, it is anti-Semitic. Second, perhaps beguiled by the fact that "spirit" is feminine in Hebrew, it identifies the Holy Spirit as a woman! Third, it contradicts a word of Jesus. That happens elsewhere in the Gnostic writings, but is very evident in the following passage from the *Gospel of Philip*:

Those who say the Lord died first and then rose up are in error, for he rose up first and then died. If one does not attain the resurrection, he will not die.

Strange stuff, but it seems to be saying that not only Jesus but all of us had pre-existence. And resurrection in the body is then redefined as our conception leading to physical birth. Only then can you die! This is a blatant denial of the teaching of the resurrection of the body as found in our Gospels and the rest of the New Testament.

Is it any wonder the church Fathers suppressed this sort of stuff as dangerous nonsense, recognising it as a completely different faith from that which Jesus had left his disciples?

The various Gnostic systems described by the Fathers differ on endless points of detail (because the Gnostic systems were so diverse), but there are at least four elements common to them all.

Firstly, there is a distinction between the unknown, transcendent and true God on the one hand and the degenerate

World-maker or Demiurge on the other, generally identified with the God of the Old Testament. The supreme God is spirit, and increasingly crass emanations led from God to this Demiurge, the author of base matter, which the Gnostics despised.

Secondly, they believed that some human beings have an affinity with God, and possess within themselves a spark of divine light imprisoned within the human body and subject, in this world, to the control of the Demiurge and his powers. The early Gnostics, like Valentinus, thought of three races of men. The lowest were the earthlings (*hylikoi*), incapable of salvation. Then there were the ordinary members of the church (*psychikoi*), strengthened by faith and good works. And then there were the *pneumatikoi*, the spiritual people (themselves, needless to say!) who have the divine spark within them and cannot decay or be harmed by material actions in the body any more than gold can be harmed by mud. Only the "spirituals" can be confident of getting to heaven.

Thirdly, all Gnostics postulated some myth or other to explain how the divine spark could reside within some people (themselves) when their physical bodies, along with the whole world, originated from an evil creature or Demiurge. This bondage of the human condition led to a longing for deliverance, which Gnosticism existed to satisfy. Needless to say, this account of the human condition was wildly different from that found in the Scriptures of the Old Testament, which is why the Gnostics as a whole rejected the Old Testament and only used quotations from it when it served their purpose.

Fourthly, all Gnostics believed in *gnosis*, knowledge (of their divine spark) as the way of salvation for the elect minority, once they had been awakened to the consciousness of their own true origin. This deliverance would mean the eventual return of the imprisoned sparks of light to their divine source. The function of Christ in this Gnostic system was to come as an emissary from the true God, to bring *gnosis* to the chosen. As a divine being, he did not assume a real human body but either inhabited it temporarily or else assumed a mere appearance of humanity.

So here we have a claim to a knowledge of God, or rather the divine spirit within the individual, as the way of salvation. There is a dualistic view of the universe, which sees the body as evil, created by an inferior deity, and the human spirit as good, created by the supreme God. From this follows naturally a disregard for the body – what matters is the soul. Needless to say, devaluing the body leads to one of two extremes. It could – and often did – produce asceticism, the attempt to mortify the body so that the soul might more readily be saved. Or else it could lead to licence, because for the true Gnostic nothing he did with his body could possibly affect the heavenly destiny of his eternal soul. So it is not surprising to find one strand of Gnostics, like the Carpocratians, indulging in wild orgies, while another, the Encratites, carried their ascetic practices to extremes.

Gnostics had a highly developed angelology which makes the mind boggle. Of course, this hierarchy of heavenly "aeons" of ever-decreasing spirituality was necessary to the system, in order to explain how a good spiritual God could have any relations at all with the inhabitants of an evil physical world.

And at the end of the day there was, of course, no resurrection of that horrible thing, the body. Instead, they looked for the release of the soul from its confines. So the immortality of the soul awaited the elite, those who had *gnosis*. Here we have a debt to Plato (c. 429–347 BC), the great Athenian philosopher, who had virtually equated goodness with knowledge.

The whole Gnostic system tended to foster an emphasis on knowledge unrelated to morality, and a sectarian exclusiveness that despised others, and formed a striking contrast to the catholicity and sanctity of primitive Christianity. It is not surprising that it drew down the wrath of the church Fathers and massive refutation by men like Irenaeus. These writers poured scorn on the Gnostics, but also made major points by way of rebuttal. Authentic Christian salvation is not merely an individual "escape from the alone to the Alone" but rather a corporate rescue by which God creates in this world a community that is an anticipatory sign of the divine purpose of healing and restoration in his world. It is not the emancipation of the soul alone but of the whole person. It is not the perquisite of an exclusive coterie, but open to one and all in Christ. And, most emphatically, real Christianity does not exempt us from the claims of either morality or charity.

This is not the place, I think, to go deeply into the variety of views found in the various Gnostic sects of the second and third centuries AD. Experts such as R.McL.Wilson, R.M. Grant, J.M. Robinson and Helmut Koester devote blameless lives to trying to elucidate the often nonsensical speculations of the Gnostics. For our purposes it is enough to realise that Irenaeus, Justin and other early church Fathers reckon that the rot set in with Simon the Magician, whom we meet in the pages of the Acts. Baptised without repenting, he never became a Christian but did become a major heretical influence and became significant enough to have a statue erected in his honour by the Emperor Claudius (AD 41–54). In addition to performing magic, he appears to have maintained that he appeared among the Jews as Son, descended in Samaria as Father, and came to the other nations as Holy Spirit!

If you think that bizarre, what do you make of Basilides, who lived in the early part of the second century? He claimed there were five primitive psychological powers: Mind, the firstborn of the ungenerated Father, and from Mind Logos, and from Logos Forethought, and from Forethought Wisdom and Power, and from Wisdom and Power the powers, archons, angels whom he calls "first", who made the first heavens. Other angels emanated from these and made another heaven like the first, and so on with copies of those above them to the total of 365, which is why the year has 365 days!

I doubt that you will want much more of this – but more there certainly is. You have only to read Irenaeus' *Against Heresies* in Robert Grant's new translation to catch the flavour of theosophy run wild. It clearly had a big appeal in the second and third centuries, since several of the leading Christians spilled a lot of ink writing against it. Until recently we had only the "refutations" put out by the orthodox writers, but since the finds at Nag Hammadi in 1945 we have a vast amount of original Gnostic material to sift through.

So now the Gnostic authors can present their material for themselves. We do not have to go to their opponents to find out what they believed. Sometimes these texts confirm what the Fathers said about them. Sometimes they correct it. But it is now more than ever obvious that the Gnostics had a fundamentally dualistic world view. They saw individuals as alienated and alone in the world. But they realised that we human beings long to return to our origin outside the world, our lost homeland.

Salvation comes by knowledge (*gnosis*) of our true condition. It is salvation *from* this world, rather than *in* this world. This world is a place to escape from, by means of secret knowledge. And in Gnosticism Jesus is generally, but not always, seen as the one who provides this knowledge. Not, as orthodox Christians taught, by his death and resurrection, and through faith in him. Not at all. Salvation in a Gnostic context comes by understanding and assimilating the secret teaching that Jesus purports to proffer in these second- and third-century documents. Mankind is trapped within the physical body, and yet the spirit is, for the true Gnostic at least, part of the divine reality. So our problem is not human sin, but human ignorance. We are like drunks who need to be sobered up, like sleepers who need to be awakened to the fact that some of us have a divine spark within us which, if brought to enlightenment, will return to heaven at the end of the day. Indeed, the Gnostic Christian is already divine, even as Jesus is divine, for both share the divine spark, even if Jesus had it to a much fuller extent.

In a word, we are saved by being the "in crowd", with superior knowledge to which ordinary Christians are blind. For the ultimate God has sent a Redeemer to bring knowledge to the trapped spirits of the elect. In Gnosticism this Redeemer is usually Jesus. But he is a divine Jesus who only appears to be human – a view which is called docetism, from the Greek word *dokein*, to appear. You could not have a divine Jesus really uniting with human nature; that would be revolting, and against the basic dualism that was central to the Gnostics. This Jesus is usually portrayed in the Gnostic texts as delivering special discourses of esoteric revelation to his followers. He does not actually die on a cross. Usually a substitute figure (i.e. a deluded human) dies there at the hands of the inferior god and his associated angels.

This emphasis on the spirit and the unimportance of the body led the Gnostics to think of themselves as the "spiritual" ones and the ordinary church members as the "soulish" ones, enslaved to the body. These might just possibly be saved, some Gnostics conceded, but only after an overwhelming array of good works, while the "spiritual ones" will be saved anyway, since they have the divine spark in them. You can see what arrogance this breeds, as well as a dangerous antinomianism, a denial of moral law, in a culture where "anything goes".

Two other aspects of Gnosticism will concern us. The first is their attitude to the Old Testament. For the most part they rejected it, seeing it as inspired by the inferior Creator God, the Demiurge. The true spiritual God could not sully his hands by creating matter. We saw this rejection of the Old Testament very clearly in Marcion in Chapter Five. The ortho- dox Christians could not tolerate this for one moment. The God who redeemed mankind is the same God who brought humanity into being and grieved over his fall. So the Old Testament is a Christian book. However, the New Testament documents were not normally seen as merely a further addi- tion to the "writings" of the Old Testament, and to be viewed as Scripture for that reason. No, they were the dynamic records of God's last Word to man, namely Jesus Christ. As we have seen, the Christian writers of the second and third centuries quote them much more than the Old Testament but do not very often refer to the New Testament documents as Scripture (*graphe*), as they regularly do to the Old. There was a wide- spread tendency in the ancient world to regard "scriptures" as hoary with age, and the Christians were agog with the new thing God had done in Jesus. His person and achievements dwarfed anything in the holy books they had taken over from Judaism. But they were keen to stress, nevertheless, that the coming of Jesus was the fulfilment of the purposes the Creator God had in mind from the dawn of time, and they would brook no separation between the God of the Old Testament and the God of the New. Neither should we!

The second aspect of Gnosticism that needs a mention is its attitude to women. The problem arises sharply in the ear- liest of the Gnostic documents that have come down to us, the *Gospel of Thomas*. Saying 114 concludes the document and reads:

Simon Peter said to them, "Let Mary leave us, for women are not worthy of life." Jesus said, "I myself shall lead her in order to make her male, so that she too may become a living spirit resembling you males. For every woman who will make herself male will enter the kingdom of heaven."

We cannot begin to understand such a saying without recognising the very different attitudes to women between the ancient world and ourselves. In antiquity women were not highly regarded, in either Greek or Jewish culture. There were glorious exceptions, but on the whole the woman was thought of as a chattel, a lower expression of being human. Women were seen as imperfect men. Imperfect in the womb because of the lack of a penis, imperfect later on because their voices did not drop and their facial hair and muscles did not develop like men's. They were indeed the weaker sex. And in a world dominated by concepts of power, inevitably women were made subordinate to men. But the ancient world saw life as a development in perfection. Plants were less perfect than animals, animals than humans, and women less perfect than men. To achieve salvation, therefore, women must pass through the next stage in perfection and become male! Listen to the first-century Jewish writer Philo: "For progress is indeed nothing else than the giving up of the female gender by changing into the male, since the female gender is material, passive, corporeal, and sense-perceptible, while the male is active, rational, incorporeal, and more akin to life and thought" (*Questions in Exodus* 1:8). Now the *Gospel of Thomas* assumes that all divine spirits will return to the place of their origin, where there will be no up and down, no male and female. But for this to happen the women must first become male. The secret knowledge that Jesus reveals produces that transformation into perfection, so that every woman who "makes herself male" by understanding and heeding his teaching will enter the kingdom.

It is curious that radical feminists are drawn to this Gnostic material, which is so anti-female and offers nothing to substantiate their cause. For example, the *Dialogue of the Saviour*, 144, represents Jesus advising the disciples to "pray in the place where there is no woman ... Destroy the works of womanhood." It is very hard for us with our political correctness to understand such an attitude, but there is no denying that it was widespread. However, the Gnostics were far from consistent in their attitudes to women. Often they were influenced by the pagan view common in the Middle East, that there is a feminine element in the divine: the male and female elements form a dyad. Thus the divine Mother appears as part of an original couple in Valentinianism, while in the *Apocryphon of John* the Holy Spirit is the feminine principle, and the *Gospel to the Hebrews* speaks of "my Mother the Spirit". Gnostic writings often use sexual symbolism to describe God. And in two of their writings, the *Gospel of Mary* and the *Gospel of Philip*, the feminine aspect is given such prominence that it assails male supremacy. These are texts that have been seized upon by books like *The Da Vinci Code* as expressing modern egalitarianism, ruthlessly suppressed by the hard-hearted male dominance of the official church. The passages concerned show a conflict between Peter, representing orthodoxy, and Mary, representing secret revelations. Peter could not believe Jesus would have bypassed him and his male colleagues and given special revelations to a woman. It is great fun for Brown, in *The Da Vinci Code*, to argue that this is all about Christ's determination to found his church on a woman, as opposed to the male succession suggested by the New Testament documents. But that is fundamentally to misunderstand the point. These late Gnostic gospels are not interested in gender roles; not even primarily in Peter and Mary. The debate is really about who receives revelation from God and who can speak in the name of authentic Christianity. And, being a Gnostic gospel, it ends, as we would expect, with Peter (i.e. orthodoxy) being rebuked and Mary (i.e. Gnosticism) being affirmed!

Such were some of the core beliefs of Gnosticism, one of the most serious heresies the church has ever faced and, as we shall see, one that is alive and well today. I debated a real live Gnostic recently on BBC Radio 4! Duncan Greenlees is a modern Gnostic and has written *The Gospel of the Gnostics*. His account of Gnosticism is highly illuminating, and shows its essential threat to the Christian faith:

> Gnosticism is a system of direct experiential knowledge of God, the Soul of the Universe. In the early centuries of this era, among a growing Christianity, it took on the form of the Christian faith, while rejecting most of its specific beliefs. Its wording is therefore largely Christian, while its spirit is that of the latest paganism of the West.

Note those final words: *its spirit is that of the latest paganism of the West.* That is a very accurate assessment.

It was the shrewdness of the early Fathers that saw the magnitude of this threat, and that is why they attacked Gnosticism so robustly, as we shall see in the next chapter.

Chapter Nine

Why Did the Church Reject the Gnostic Gospels?

e knew a bit about the Gnostic material from fragments mentioned by ancient writers, or from stri-
dent denunciations from the orthodox, but the
story really began in 1945. And it is as significant for understanding the developments in Christianity as the discovery in
1947 of the Dead Sea Scrolls was for those in Judaism.

Mohammed Ali and six of his Bedouin friends were dig-
ging for *sabakh*, a sort of fertiliser, near the cliffs called Jabal
al-Tarif alongside the Nile in Upper Egypt. Across the river
was the largest village in the area, Nag Hammadi, some 300
miles south of Cairo and 40 miles north of Luxor.
Mohammed's younger brother struck something hard
beneath the surface. It was a skeleton. And next to it was a
great big jar, which they dug up. At first reluctant to open the
sealed jar, for fear of *djinn*, they eventually did open it in the
hope of buried treasure. They were disappointed to find only
thirteen old leather-bound books, which were of little use to
them since they could not read.

Ali took the books home and left them in an outhouse,
and that evening his mother used some of them to light the
fire. Events were a little obscure after that, but skulduggery
and even murder were part of the mix. In due course the
books ended up with a Coptic priest, whose brother-in-law

was a teacher and realised the books might be valuable. They were sold to the Coptic Museum. Eventually an international team was assembled to photograph, study, translate and print them, under the direction of the American scholar James Robinson. They can now be acquired in a single volume, *The Nag Hammadi Library* edited by James Robinson.

Two paramount questions arise. Are these documents important, and what did they contain?

They certainly are important. They constitute one of the most important finds of modern times. They bring to light books that have been unseen for over 1,500 years. The twelve leather-bound books and parts of a thirteenth contain 52 works, six of which are duplicates. The books are all Gnostic or Encratite. There is not a single orthodox Christian book among them. The jar of books was placed there shortly before 400 AD. Maybe they were the treasured library of one of the Gnostic monasteries, hidden for protection. Indeed, when we recall that the Bishop of Alexandria, Athanasius, wrote a letter to the churches of Egypt setting out very clear limits to the canon of Scripture in the year 367 AD, and insisting that heretical books should not be read, then it is all too possible that Gnostic monks, who were doubtless fond of their collection, hid them away in the sands in the hope that a more liberal rule might in due course emerge! We do not know. In any event, the pages are made of papyrus and written in Coptic. But the Coptic shows clear evidence of having been translated, sometimes very inaccurately or with large gaps, from Greek originals, which will have been a good deal earlier. For example, from previous discoveries we have fragments of the *Gospel of Thomas* in Greek that come from the end of the second century.

The contents of this library are immensely varied. We have five non-canonical gospels, namely the *Gospels of Thomas*,

Philip, Truth, the Egyptians and *Mary*. There is a *Treatise on the Resurrection,* a supposed *Prayer of Paul,* strange stuff like the *Exegesis of the Soul,* the *Dialogue of the Saviour,* two *Apocalypses of James,* a bit of Plato's *Republic,* and the *Three Steles of Seth!* A massive body of literature has grown up around these documents. Remember that they are late (hundreds of years after the New Testament writings), Gnostic, very incomplete, and in style, world view and content miles away from the Christianity that we meet in the New Testament. There will be room in this chapter only to look at the ones that have caused most controversy, or which have provided a platform for a revisionist version of Christianity.

The Gospel of Thomas

Undoubtedly the most important is the *Gospel of Thomas.* The first thing to realise is that this is not a gospel at all, as we know it. It has no theme, no actions of Jesus, no crucifixion, no resurrection. It is simply a collection of 114 sayings of Jesus. More than half the sayings in the *Gospel of Thomas* bear some similarity to sayings in our Gospels. In a number of instances the similarity is close. Other sayings start like our Gospels but continue in a strange way. One such is no.2, "Jesus said Let him who seeks continue until he finds. When he finds, he will be troubled. When he becomes troubled he will be astonished, and he will rule over the All." "The All" is a Gnostic idea and evokes a lot of interest in the Nag Hammadi writings.

Then there are very strange sayings which clearly have a Gnostic thrust, such as Saying 22. In answer to the question of the disciples, "Shall we as children enter the kingdom?", Jesus is made to reply:

> When you make the two one, and when you make the inside like the outside and the outside like the inside, and the above like the below, and when you make the male and the female one and the same, so that the male be not male nor the female female; and when you fashion eyes in the place of an eye, and a hand in the place of a hand, and a foot in the place of a foot, and a likeness in the place of a likeness, then you will enter the kingdom.

This appears to be alluding to the view of many Gnostics that mankind will one day be reunited into an androgynous figure, a widespread Gnostic hope. "Many who are first will become last and they will become one and the same" (Saying 4) is somewhat similar and points to the divine realm where there is no conflict or diversity, but only the restoration of original unity. The reference to the "heaven above the heaven" (Saying 11) suggests a Gnostic cosmology, as does the reference about coming from the light (Saying 50). "I disclose my mysteries to those who are worthy of my mysteries" (Saying 62) betrays typical Gnostic arrogance, so markedly different from the biblical teaching that none of us are worthy. "There is a light within a man and he lights up the whole world" (Saying 24) indicates its Gnostic provenance: Christology has become anthropology! A commonplace in Gnostic writings is criticism of the world as drunk (Saying 28) and in poverty (Sayings 3 and 29). Of all the sayings in the *Gospel of Thomas* that reveal a Gnostic background, Saying 28 takes pride of place:

> Jesus said "I took my place in the midst of the world, and I appeared to them in flesh. I found all of them intoxicated: I found none of them thirsty. And my soul became afflicted for the sons of men, because they are blind in their hearts and do not have sight; for empty they came into the world and empty

too they seek to leave the world. But for the moment they are intoxicated. When they shake off their wine, they will repent."

This saying, of all those in the *Gospel of Thomas*, is the one that most clearly offers us the traditional Gnostic Redeemer myth. His coming is meant to wake up some of them (the elect!) and bring them to self-knowledge.

This Gnostic collection of sayings of Jesus reminds one of "Q", the source scholars have postulated to explain the similarity in the sayings of Jesus in Matthew and Luke that are absent from Mark. Like "Q" *Thomas* is a sayings source. Some of them are very likely to be genuine, but there can be little doubt that this particular collection is heavily tarred with a Gnostic brush. The Gnosticism is presupposed rather than heavily stressed, but the provenance is not in doubt.

Many on the fringes of New Testament scholarship seek to lionise the *Gospel of Thomas* as if it were some early testimony to Jesus which the four Gospels have eclipsed. They draw attention to similarities between *Thomas* and "Q". But in so doing they destroy their case. For "Q", if it ever existed, was valued simply as a collection of Jesus' teachings, never as an alternative gospel. For the good news about Jesus, sent from God to bring us salvation through his death and resurrection, could never be adequately represented by a mere collection of his sayings. The very existence of the four Gospels, with their massive emphasis on his death and resurrection, did not merely embody the essential tenets of the new faith but excluded less-than-adequate expressions of that faith. That is why "Q" never was, nor could have been, retained as it stood, but only as incorporated in the fuller and adequate Gospels of Matthew and Luke, which included the saving acts of Jesus' cross and resurrection. And if the sayings source "Q" never attained the status of a recognised gospel, we can be sure that the sayings source *Thomas* never did either. In point of fact it is much later than the Gospels, being written some time in the middle or latter part of the second century, with its only full surviving text coming from the end of the fourth. It is clearly secondary to our Gospels because it knows them and several of the letters of Paul. In *Thomas* salvation does not come through Jesus' cross and resurrection but through *gnosis*, knowing your true identity – if you happen to be one of the "spiritual" ones. The physical world is not, as we read in the Bible, basically good though marred by sin and suffering. It is corrupt and worthless: "Whoever has come to understand the world has found only a corpse, and whoever has found a corpse is superior to the world" (Saying 56). Salvation means escaping the constraints of the body, which has trapped the divine spark of our eternal souls. The kingdom of God is not God's rescue for rebellious sinners but "the kingdom of God is within you." It is entirely spiritual and internal. It is all about realising who you are and escaping from the constraints of this evil, worthless world. And it is Jesus who can provide this knowledge, that the human spirit (of the elect!) is divine, as divine as Jesus and made one with Jesus: "He who will drink from my mouth will become like me. I myself shall become he, and the things that are hidden will be revealed to him" (Saying 108). Jesus brings the true knowledge needed by the inner spirit in order to be released from the flesh and reunited with the heavenly realm from which it came. And so, as the sharpest Saying (42) of the *Gospel* puts it, "Become passers by".

Elaine Pagels, one of the scholars who has greatest sympathy with the outlook of the *Gospel of Thomas*, acknowledges that the religion there described is utterly different from what we find in the Gospels. She says, as she compares the message of St John's Gospel with that of *Thomas*:

Thomas's Jesus directs each disciple to discover the light within ("within a person of light there is light"), but John's Jesus declares instead that "I am the light of the world" and that "whoever does not come to me walks in darkness." In Thomas Jesus reveals to the disciples that "you are from the kingdom and to it you shall return" and teaches them to say for themselves that "we come from the light." But John's Jesus speaks as the only one who comes "from above" and so has rightful priority over everyone else. "You are from below; I am from above... The one who comes from above is above all." (Elaine Pagels, *Beyond Belief: The Secret Gospel of Thomas*, p. 68).

Two different worlds, are they not? One rooted in human potential, the other rooted in the person and work of the divine Jesus.

Three Gnostic texts

It will be helpful to take three texts together, because they give clear insight into one of the main teachings of the Gnostics, even of those who believed in a divine Redeemer. In a word, they regarded Jesus as so divine that he could not have been truly human. He came from the good God of light, and could not have been corrupted by a human body that originated from the inferior deity, the Demiurge, who made the material world. So Jesus only appeared to be human. And he only appeared to die on the cross.

In the *Acts of John* 93, John is talking to his fellow disciples:

Sometimes when I meant to touch him I met a material, solid body; but at other times again when I felt him, his substance was immaterial and incorporeal ... as if it did not exist at all.

He goes on to say that Jesus did not even leave any footprints. He was an apparition.

If his incarnation was unreal, so was his crucifixion. While the crucifixion is going on Jesus stands in the middle of a cave on the Mount of Olives, and gives light to it and says, "John, for the people below in Jerusalem I am being crucified and pierced with lances and reeds and given vinegar and gall to drink. But to you I am speaking, and listen to what I say. I put into your mind to come up to this mountain so that you may hear what a disciple should learn from his teacher and a man of God" (*Acts of John* 97). A similar account appears in the *Apocalypse of Peter*, 81, one of the Gnostic documents from Nag Hammadi. Once again we find this docetic understanding of Jesus: he was not really human. Peter is speaking:

> I saw him apparently being seized by them. And I said "What am I seeing, O Lord? Is it really you whom they are taking? And are you holding on to me? And are they hammering the hands and feet of someone else? Who is this one on the tree who is glad and laughing?"

Then comes Jesus' stunning reply:

> He whom you saw on the tree, glad and laughing, this is the living Jesus. But he into whose hands and feet they are driving the nails is his fleshly part, his substitute. They are putting to shame that which is in his likeness. But look at him – and look at me!'

It is very clear what the author of this book is saying. The body is just a shell, made by the creator of this world. The true self is within and cannot be touched by physical pain. Those who don't have this knowledge think they can kill Jesus. But the divine, immortal Jesus laughs them to scorn.

A third document from the Gnostic hoard at Nag Hammadi makes the same point. Jesus is speaking:

> It was another ... who drank the gall and vinegar; it was not I ... It was another, Simon, who carried the cross on his shoulders. It was another on whom they placed the crown of thorns. But I was rejoicing in the height over all the riches of the archons ... laughing at their ignorance ... for I kept changing my forms above, transforming them from appearance to appearance. (*Second Treatise of the Great Seth*, 56ff)

This was clearly Gnostic stock in trade. It is found in Basilides about 140 AD, who recounts that while Simon of Cyrene carried Jesus' cross, Jesus himself pulled off a supernatural switch, swapping appearances with Simon, so that the Romans crucified the wrong man. Meanwhile Jesus stood by, laughing (see Irenaeus, *Against Heresies* 1:24).

It is ironic that, in *The Da Vinci Code*, Dan Brown gets all this spectacularly wrong. He maintains that the Gnostic gospels were the originals and that they were suppressed by a corrupt Catholic Church which instead presented us with the four Gospels as we know them – which are supposed to have divinised the original human Jesus. But the Gnostic gospels do not give us an earthy, human Jesus at all, but the complete opposite: an ethereal, divine Jesus, far removed from the pains and mortality of this world! Brown is equally far removed from the truth!

You may ask, why should these ancient debates about Jesus' true humanity matter? Well, there is an overwhelming answer. The false teaching of these Gnostics has influenced the Qur'an. Muhammad seems to have picked up from the degenerate Christians of his day this Gnostic idea that Jesus never really died but that someone else died in his stead.

"They said in boast, 'We killed Christ Jesus the Son of Mary, the apostle of God'. But they killed him not, nor crucified him, but so it was made to appear to them ... Of a surety they killed him not" (Qur'an 4:157). Muslim commentators have traditionally interpreted this verse to mean that Jesus was not crucified. Either Judas or Simon of Cyrene was substituted in his place, while he was taken up alive into heaven. And so this Gnostic error lives on, in the beliefs of more than a billion Muslims, to this present day.

Of course, the view that Jesus was so divine that he could not be human produced the opposite heresy – i.e., he was so human that he could not be divine. This was the position adopted by the Ebionites, a sect of Jewish Christians whom we first meet in the second century. Sadly, none of their writings survive, not even in Nag Hammadi, but it is clear from church Fathers such as Irenaeus and Origen that they did not believe that Jesus was the Son of God. He was flesh and blood like the rest of us, the child of Joseph and Mary. But because he kept the whole of the Jewish law perfectly, the Spirit came upon him at his baptism and God adopted him to be his Son. Like the orthodox, they seem to have believed that Jesus went to the cross for the sins of the whole world, and that God the Father vindicated him by raising him from the dead. But their history is very obscure and certainty about their views is impossible.

It is not surprising that many people could not conceive how Jesus could be both human and divine. Was this not a contradiction in terms? The answer given by those who knew him, and whose testimony is recorded in the New Testament, is that this is no contradiction. Indeed, it is a divine necessity. If Jesus was really to be the redeemer of mankind as well as the revealer of God, he needed to share the nature of both. If he was to prove a bridge over the troubled water that separated sinful humanity from a holy God, he had to be a bridge firmly grounded on both sides of that water. He had to be both human and divine. And why should an omnipotent God not be able in his great love to shrink himself to share our humanity? The Gospels affirm that he did. That is why Christians have worshipped him in awe and wonder for two millennia. We see perhaps the earliest manifestation of this conviction and this worship in the hymn Paul quotes in his letter to the Philippians, written probably in the mid-50s AD. Speaking of Jesus, he says, "who, though he was in the form of God, did not regard equality with God as something to be held onto, but emptied himself, taking the form of a slave, being born in human likeness" (Philippians 2:6, 7).

The Gospels of Philip and Mary

The Gospel of Philip, which appears to be a collection of excerpts from other Gnostic works, was probably compiled early in the third century. It is certainly much later than the New Testament, from which it makes several quotations. It is full of puzzling sayings, about the sacraments, the "man-eating God", the world that came into being by mistake, the mystery of the bridal chamber, and so on. It has a very different world view even from the *Gospel of Thomas*, let alone that of the four Gospels. A bizarre work like this would not have come into the public consciousness at all, were it not for Dan Brown's citation of the *Gospel of Philip* in *The Da Vinci Code*:

> The companion of the Saviour is Mary Magdalene. But Christ loved her more than all the disciples and used to kiss her often on her mouth. The rest of the disciples were offended by it and expressed disapproval. They said to him "Why do you love her more than all of us?" The Saviour answered and said to them "Why do I not love you like her?"

Incidentally there is a good deal of guesswork here. The Coptic text is full of gaps. It reads:

> And the companion of the [...] Mary Magdalene. [...] loved her more than [all?] the disciples [and used to?] kiss her [often?] on her [...] The rest of [the disciples ... ?] They said to him "Why do you love her more than all of us?" The Saviour answered and said to them "Why do I not love you like her? When a blind man and one who sees are both in darkness they are no different from one another. When the light comes, then he who sees will see the light, and he who is blind will remain in darkness."

Something rather similar appears in the so-called *Gospel of Mary* (the text is in disarray and it does not even have a title). The Coptic text recovered from Nag Hammadi is late fourth-century, but part of the text is found in a single page of Greek papyrus of the third century – and they do not match! It is about Mary Magdalene and her special vision of the ascent of the soul through the various heavens until it achieves its goal, final rest. A very Gnostic theme. It concerns secret knowledge, which Peter asks her to reveal: "Sister, we know that the Saviour loved you more than the rest of women. Tell us the words of the Saviour which you remember but ... which we have not heard." Mary answers, "What is hidden from you I will proclaim to you." She does – at length! When she has finished, Andrew is highly sceptical: "I do not believe that the Saviour said this. For certainly these teachings are strange ideas." Peter's view is the same. "Did he really speak privately with a woman without our knowledge and not openly ? Are we to turn around and all listen to her? Did he prefer her to us?" Mary weeps, and denies she is lying. Then Levi takes Mary's side. "Peter, you have always been hot-tempered. Now I see you are contending against the woman like an adversary. But if the Saviour made her worthy, who are you indeed to reject her?" Levi continues by urging his colleagues to "put on the perfect man" (i.e. the perfect divine human being within them) and to proclaim this as the "gospel" throughout the world.

From these tenuous references in documents centuries later than the New Testament, Dan Brown makes several gross assumptions. Jesus was the lover of Mary Magdalene. He married her. Jesus was the original feminist. He entrusted his church not to Peter but to Mary Magdalene. It is not worth discussing the even more way-out suggestions that he claims as truth, namely that together they spawned a royal race, which held sway in France, and that Mary Magdalene was herself the Holy Grail!

Now Brown is no scholar. But Professors Elaine Pagels and Karen King are, and it is their views that lie behind Dan Brown. Elaine Pagels confesses to being a Gnostic herself. In her book *Beyond Belief*, she tells how she became alienated from historic Christianity, but retained a great interest in the study of the early church. While doing doctoral work at Harvard she suddenly found a sentence from the *Gospel of Thomas* affecting her powerfully. It was this: "If you bring forth what is within you, what you bring forth will save you." Her comment is fascinating. "The strength of this saying is that it does not tell us what to believe but challenges us to discover what lies hidden within our selves; and with a shock of recognition I realised that his perspective seemed to me to be self-evidently true." In other words, Professor Pagels apparently ranks herself among the Gnostics.

Professor King's feminist perspective equally seems to govern her conclusions. She is the author of *The Gospel of Mary of Magdala: Jesus and the First Woman Apostle*. And she is concerned to champion women in leadership. She complains that "the apostles were considered to be guarantors of the true teaching of the church, and male bishops continued to be their sole legitimate successors. This male model of discipleship also provided (and continues to provide) a rationale for the exclusion of women from leadership roles, ignoring the presence of women disciples through Jesus' ministry, at the crucifixion, and as the first witnesses of the resurrection."

Her feminism attracts her towards the position given to Mary in these two ancient texts, and to Hippolytus' description of Mary Magdalene as a "female apostle". King is right in asserting that the attitude of Jesus to women was revolutionary: in contrast to the prejudices of those days, Jesus viewed them with great respect, as our Gospels make clear. The women were the last to leave him at the cross and the first to meet him after the resurrection. Mary and the others were sent by the risen Christ to tell the other disciples that he was risen (Mark 16:7). Thus Mary Magdalene was, in the proper sense of the word, an apostle ("sent one") to the disciples. And that is how Hippolytus, writing early in the third century, sees her.

His words are significant. "Lest the female apostles should doubt the angels, Christ himself came to them so that the women would be apostles of Christ ... Christ showed himself to the (male) apostles and said to them 'It is I who appeared to these women and I wanted to send them to you as apostles.'" Hippolytus rightly affirms Mary and her women colleagues in their role of witnesses to the resurrection, but neither she nor they were ever given any official leadership role in the subsequent church. King's mistake is to impose a twenty-first-century concept on ancient documents. Jesus did value women, and he valued men too. But he did not espouse the restrictive cause of a fully fledged feminist.

A glance at the work of Pagels and King shows the contemporary academic use being made of these old Coptic texts. But, as we indicated earlier, the evidence does not bear the weight laid upon it by either of them, let alone by Brown. The *Gospels of Philip* and *Mary* are not about eroticism (kissing, by the way, was normal and non-sexual in the ancient church – see 1 Corinthians 16:20; 1 Peter 5:14), nor about feminism. They are concerned with the source of divine revelation. Gnostics who argued for secret esoteric revelations saw themselves as the downtrodden female (Mary) being abused by the hot-tempered male (Peter). It was a struggle about the true meaning of Christianity. Was its content determined by the New Testament Scriptures to which the church Fathers appealed, or by the secret revelations to which the Gnostics laid claim? And it was that momentous issue that makes the *Gospel of Philip* and the *Gospel of Mary* worth reading.

Chapter Ten

What's So Wrong with Gnosticism Anyway?

A word with two meanings

Many of the orthodox writings that have survived from the second and third centuries contain strong, vitriolic attacks on Gnosticism. They clearly saw it as a major enemy of the faith brought to them in the New Testament, which they tried to guard. But what was so wrong with it, in their eyes, that it merited such a strong and sustained assault from so many quarters?

In order to answer this important question we need to retrace our steps a little. We drew attention in an earlier chapter to the scholarly debates surrounding Gnosticism. Was it a pre-Christian phenomenon, which had bits of Christianity grafted on to it? Or was it an early Christian deviation? The jury is still out on this question, largely because the word "Gnostic" is used in two ways. In one sense it applies to a dozen or more specific theosophical sects in the second and third centuries which broke off relations with the church – and with each other! Let us use the capital letter for them, Gnostic. But there is a much looser usage of the term, to denote a sort of vague syncretistic religiosity, widely diffused in the Middle East, which existed independently of and prior to Christianity. In the following discussion we will use the lower case for that, gnostic.

Many of the raw materials that went to make up second-century Gnosticism were around before Christ. There was the dualism drawn from Zoroastrianism, elements of speculative Judaism, material derived (at some remove) from Plato, and the whole ensemble was mixed up with myths, astrology and magic, which were seen as the best techniques for overcoming the dark powers of fate, and achieving salvation.

This was the air you breathed in the Graeco-Roman world into which the gospel spread in the first century AD, once it hatched from its Jewish shell. Here, even the God of the Hebrews had been welcomed into the polytheism of the day, and had been identified with Dionysus or Saturn! Myths of a divine redeemer figure coming to open the eyes of the elect and give them a password to eternal rest may have been circulating in the first century. They certainly were very shortly after. So when the Christians proclaimed that the divine redeemer had been born in Judaea, had been crucified under Pilate, had risen again, and would come on the last day to judge the world, there were plenty of parallels to many of these ideas in pagan mythology. But parallels with a difference. For Christianity was not about myths but about a historical figure, and one whom lots of people still alive had known! That was the claim that truly amazed the ancient world. Here were men and women enthusiastically maintaining that these age-old longings had actually been achieved by a recent historical figure. How much easier it would have been if these stories could be cut free from the historical basis and turned back into psychological myths that belonged in the Mystery Cults! That is what the Gnostics wanted to do. But that is what the Christians steadfastly refused to allow. Theirs was not the one mystery cult that happened to succeed. It was the good news of a living God who had come to offer mankind salvation by the sacrifice of himself on a cross.

Early gnosticism in New Testament days

Although developed systems of Gnosticism certainly belong to the second century and not earlier, the tendencies are already being addressed in the New Testament itself. This is particularly obvious in the writings of Paul and John. In order to understand what was wrong with gnostic ideas, we could not do better than start with these apostolic writings.

At Corinth, for example, there was a spiritual aristocracy who prided themselves on a superior wisdom and deeper mystical experiences than other Christians, and even than the apostle himself. They believed they had already achieved perfection and looked down on their inferior Christian brothers and sisters. They were also dualists, who believed that the spirit was good and the body and material things either indifferent or actually evil. As we saw earlier, once you hold this view about the body it tends to lead to two opposite patterns of behaviour. Some of them advocated an asceticism so extreme that husbands and wives refrained from sex and engaged couples did not get married. Others went in for an advanced sexual anarchy and seem to have regarded the sacraments as magical guarantees of salvation. Nothing you did with your body could affect your eternal bliss. They also rejected the Hebrew doctrine of the resurrection of the body, seemingly preferring Plato's teaching about the immortality of the soul. In any case, what could resurrection of any kind add to those who had already "arrived" and were perfect?

The situation had developed further by the time Paul wrote to the Colossians nearly ten years later. The bucolic Colossians were besieged by people claiming a superior wisdom, indeed a philosophy that far transcended ordinary Christian experience. They were encouraged to worship angelic powers, which were identified with the heavenly bodies. Mystic initiation rites were advocated, and an amalgam of immoral practices on the one hand and strict asceticism on the other, along with feast days drawn from the Jewish calendar. All of this was designed to free the soul for its ascent through the principalities and powers to union with the divine.

It is instructive to see how St Paul dealt with these views, which obviously have close affinities with later Gnosticism in the developed sense of that word.

In writing to the Corinthians, Paul insists that he is not one of the wandering sophist teachers of the day, advocating a higher wisdom: his concentration is on Jesus Christ, crucified. Jesus, not some theosophical construct, is the wisdom of God. Nor are his Corinthian believers a coterie of aristocrats born with silver spoons in their mouths. They come from all walks of life, and have been transformed by the power of the risen Jesus. As for the resurrection, it matters enormously that this is *bodily* resurrection. The Lord is for the body – something no Gnostic could say. Of course he is: for he is the Creator who designed the body in the first place, came and indwelt the human body, and died and rose in the body. And for this reason the body is sacred, and not to be sullied with immorality. But marriage is a gift of God, and so is singleness. Neither is superior to the other. Already you see that Paul and his gnostic opponents are practising a different religion.

His treatment in Colossians is more systematic and more trenchant. He identifies and rebuts four major errors in the positions of these proto-gnostics.

Doctrine
Their teaching robbed Christ of his unique place in creation (Colossians 1:15–17) and redemption (Colossians 1:18–20). Once you believe that matter is evil you have to postulate a

chain of progressively more physical intermediaries between a good God and a bad world. Christ, in their system, so it appears, was just one of those mediators, alongside the "thrones, dominions, principalities and authorities". Paul's reply is that whatever spiritual forces there may be were created for Christ and by Christ. He is both prior to and sovereign over (*prototokos* – a technical term, 1:15) all things, and he alone is the principle of coherence in the world, the one who holds the laws of nature in place (Colossians 1:17, 18).

Did these early gnostics teach the efficacy of angelic mediators in redemption? Paul replies that the creator of the world is the head of the church (Colossians 1:15, 18). It was he alone who made reconciliation (1:20). Indeed, in him alone all the fulness of the Godhead has its lasting manifestation – and moreover in bodily form (2:9)! The Greek expression used here is explosive. It would have driven the gnostics to apoplexy! Paul even uses one of their favourite words, *pleroma* (the "fulness", contributed to by the collaboration of all the angelic powers), and throws it back at them. Christ has all the fulness of the Godhead – and so angelic mediators are futile. The false teachers aimed at making a *partial* reconciliation between God and man through angelic intervention, but they were ineffective because they were neither human nor divine, and therefore could not span the gulf between God and man. Christ offers a *complete* reconciliation since he is both human and divine, in solidarity with both parties, and by his death he brings them back together (Colossians 1:20). This is the complete rebuttal of the "Jesus and…" heresy, as common now as it was then.

Morals

As we have already seen, once you regard matter as suspect or positively evil, you can either abuse it or mortify it: it makes no difference, since it cannot affect the destiny of your divine soul. In Colossians 2:16–23 Paul attacks the false asceticism of the first lot, and in 3:1–17 the licentiousness of the second group. The asceticism (which might look so impressive) is attacked partly because it is powerless to curb the lusts of the flesh (Colossians 2:23), but mainly because it springs from the wrong view that the body is evil and the spirit good. On the contrary, the body is neutral, and the spirit corrupt: the "old nature" has to be put off (3:9)! For both ascetics and libertines Paul's practical conclusion is the same. They must die with Christ (3:5) instead of mortifying some of their members – or, alternatively, abusing them. They must rise with Christ (3:1ff) and set their affections not on earthly precepts – or, alternatively, sensual enjoyment – but above, where Christ is. Thus they will be renewed in the image of their Creator (3:10), who is no low-grade Demiurge but the God and Father of Jesus Christ, the Sovereign Lord who made mankind in his image. This teaching, too, is very relevant today. Christians do not normally need deliverance from dark powers in order to counter bad habits, but they do need to learn more of the dying and rising life that is implicit in their baptism and which is the route to spiritual maturity.

Social life

The exclusiveness of the "know-all" crowd compromised the universality of the gospel. There is no room for colour, class or caste among believers (Colossians 3:11). Christ is all, and in them all, if they are Christians. That is why Paul stresses that there is indeed a Christian mystery, but it is an open mystery in contrast to the secret rites of the gnostics (1:26). That is why he teaches wisdom to all, and strives to present everyone (not some gnostic elite) "perfect" in Christ (1:28). Remember that the mysteries, esoteric knowledge and perfection were regarded in gnostic circles as the perquisite of the elect few. Paul's social concern for the quality of love and fellowship among believers explains why he is so keen to see love and mutual submission among husbands and wives, children, employers and employees. The is no room for a secret society among Christians: that is the main reason why Freemasonry is wrong. Christ brings to light the "mystery", hidden down the ages, but revealed through the gospel, that the despised Gentiles could be fellow heirs with God's people the Jews, without any discrimination. And nothing could be more anti-gnostic than that!

Spirituality

But Paul has not finished his critique. He is concerned with the warped spirituality of these early gnostics. Their emphasis on philosophical knowledge (Colossians 2:8) implied a Platonism ("nobody wilfully sins") which is far removed from the Christian recognition that sin is an integral part of human life. And that is why Paul reiterates the need to have Christ dwelling in their lives: "Christ in you, the hope of glory" (1:27). Only he can redeem them and proffer them forgiveness of sins (1:14). Once again, Paul's critique goes to the heart of much of our contemporary error. Spiritual regeneration, not mere intellectual improvement; conversion, not self-effort; a new heart, not merely a puffed-up mind – this is where real Christianity begins.

The first letter of John has to deal with various manifestations of the same gnostic world view, and John combats them as vigorously as St Paul, incidentally emphasising that he was a personal eyewitness of Jesus, and so bears true witness to him (1 John 1:1–3). Once again we find the *doctrinal* problem. Some were teaching that Jesus was not the Christ (2:22). They claimed to know the Father without the Son (2:23). They denied that Jesus had come in the flesh (4:1–3). They taught that he came by water but not by blood (5:6–8).

Clearly, another error was *ethical*. They taught that you could be righteous without doing righteousness (1 John 3:7), that you could know God without keeping his word (1 John 2:4, 5), that you could abide in God without walking like Christ (2:6). Sin was unreal (1:6), already eradicated (1:8), or something they had never indulged in (1:10). There was plenty of talk of light (as in the later Gnostics) but it was an "enlightenment" that emancipated them from the claims of morality.

They were sorely adrift, too, on the *social* level. They considered themselves an elite, and as a result both despised Christian brethren and flirted with "the world" (1 John 2:9–11, 15–17). John robustly denounces these deceivers, who by the time he writes seem to have separated themselves from orthodox Christians (2:26; 2:19), but the poison of their teaching was still around.

To find a background for all this we need to find a system that both denied that Jesus was the Son or the Christ who had come in the flesh, and also regarded holiness and love as matters of indifference. The church Fathers rightly saw this in the teaching of Cerinthus, one of the very earliest Gnostics in the full sense of the word. Cerinthus sought to sever the man Jesus from the heavenly Christ: born as the child of Joseph and Mary, the divine Christ came upon Jesus at his baptism and left him before Calvary. To which John, the eyewitness and apostle, replies that Jesus Christ is one person, that he is

God's Son, and that he passed through both baptism and death, water and blood (1 John 5:6). Cerinthus' morals were highly suspect (an early tradition recounts that John once ran from the baths when he realised Cerinthus was there too, lest the roof fall in!), and John has to rebut his immorality (1 John 3:3, 9 and 3:6, 7). Finally, countering the elitism and lovelessness of his opponents, John reminds his readers that they *all* have knowledge, *all* have God's anointing (2:13ff., cf. 5:20). And *all* are called to love the brethren, the proof of being in touch with God who is love (4:7, 8). How could you get more anti-gnostic than that?

Realising the danger of this heresy, John sets to work to rebut it forcefully, and he does so very skilfully. He is concerned to set forth the true nature of Christianity over against a sinister deception. The truth that sets you free has three aspects: true belief, true behaviour, and true love.

Let's start with *true belief*. Does it matter what we believe about Jesus? If we have God, why bother with Jesus?

John is convinced that if Jesus does not share God's very nature, it robs his person of its dignity, his teaching of its authority, and his death of its efficacy. So he insists on the importance of right belief. Jesus is the Christ (1 John 5:1), the Son of God (5:5). He came both by water and by blood (5:6). His death dealt with sins (2:2). If you have Christ, you have new life; if not, you don't (5:11, 12).

Moreover, John appeals to his own unparalleled intimacy with the historical Jesus, and bases his testimony on that (1 John 1:1–4). And finally he alludes to the sacraments (5:6, 8). If physical things are evil, how about the sacraments?

St John, it seems to me, gets this worked up about true belief for three good reasons. Without Christ coming in the flesh we are left with an unknown God. Without Christ dying on the cross we are left with an unattainable God. Without

Christ risen to new life, we are offered no joy or peace, only an absentee God.

Second, John turns to *true behaviour*. Can you be righteous without doing righteousness? No (1 John 3:7). Can you know God without obeying his word? No (2:4, 5). Can you abide in God without walking like Christ? No again (2:6). As for sin, some said it was all imaginary (1:6), some that it was eradicated in superior believers like themselves (1:8), and some affirmed that they had never sinned (1:10). But John will have none of it. One crucial test of true Christianity is that it must show. The only proof that I am righteous is that I act righteously (3:7); that I am born of God is if I do not habitually sin (3:9, 19); that I know God is if I obey him (2:3); that I abide in him is if I conform to the lifestyle of Jesus (2:6). John nails their Enlightenment idea of light as well (1:5–7). Since God is light, we must walk in the light. The criterion of mysticism must be ethical.

The third strand John adduces for his rebuttal of the gnostics of his day is much the same as Paul's. There must be *true love* in authentic Christianity. He answers their snobbery, their loveless assumption that they are better than others, very pungently. God is love. He did not keep himself in cold isolation from humankind (4:9). The God who is light is the God who is love. So must his children be (3:11–18; 4:7–12). How then can they hate brother Christians (2:11) and neglect the poor and needy (3:16–18)? In 4:20, 21 his argument comes to a climax: "This [is the] commandment [that] we have from him, that he who loves God should love his brother also." Far from being a mark of superiority, loveless pride is a sign of the anti-God spirit (4:8).

Needless to say, when there is real love for God in the human heart we always find its counterpart: "do not love the world" (1 John 2:15–17). "The world" in John's letters denotes human society that remains at odds with God. And it is marked by the three characteristics that appear in the fall of man as told in Genesis 3: the lust of the flesh, the lust of the eyes, and the pride of life. These are the very opposite of love, and unfortunately they had infected the church. Love is crucial among the people of God. Worldliness is abhorrent. John writes to emphasise the priority of true belief, holiness and love in contrast to his opponents. And in his second letter, after reiterating "the coming of Jesus Christ in the flesh", he warns them against even listening to anyone who holds "advanced views" and does not remain in the teaching of Christ (2 John 9). Of such a one he says "Do not receive him into the house or give him any greeting; for he who greets him shares his wicked work" (2 John 10–11). The situation is plain. Towards the end of the first century, gnostic tendencies were such a danger to the church membership that total separation was the only answer.

These, then, are the three strands that are woven into all parts of the Johannine letters. The truth that sets men free is marked by true belief, true behaviour and true love. By way of summary, 1 John 5:1–3 brings the three together. "Every one who *believes* that Jesus is the Christ is a child of God, and every one who *loves* the parent loves the child. By this we know that we love the children of God, when we love God and *obey* his commandments. For this is the love of God, that we keep his commandments – and his commandments are not burdensome." John has arraigned his gnostic opponents on each of these three areas, critical to Christianity – belief, behaviour, and love. And he has found them wanting. That is what was wrong with the whole gnostic movement. It still is in their modern successors.

After the apostolic age

In the sub-apostolic age there was a great deal of writing against the Gnostics, but nothing that went deeper than the treatment that had already been outlined by Paul and John. In the early part of the second century we do not find men like these towering intellects of the New Testament period. Perhaps there was an anti-intellectualism abroad. Had not Paul warned the Colossians to "see to it that no-one makes a prey of you by philosophy and vain deceit, according to human traditions, according to the elemental spirits of the universe, and not according to Christ"? (Colossians 2:8). It would have been natural enough for the ordinary Christians of the early second century to steer well clear of all philosophy, especially since it became a major feature in the Gnostic systems. I guess they thought it was of the devil! Indeed, we know they did, for Hippolytus, writing at the very end of the second century and into the third, constructs his book *Refutation of All Heresies* (of which seven volumes still exist) on the assumption that each of the Gnostic sects has been led astray by some philosopher!

But by the time we encounter Justin, Clement and Irenaeus later in the second century we find major intellectuals who are able to do battle with the heretics on their own ground. Justin, for example, argues that the Stoics are excellent in their ethical teaching, but disastrously wrong in their fatalism, pantheism and materialism. He has quite a positive evaluation of Platonic thought, which was his pre-Christian background, but is resolutely biblical in his view of God and God's dealings with the world. His strong biblical core enables him not only to approve the good things in Greek philosophy but to pass judgment on the bad. The second book of Irenaeus' *Against the Heresies* is devoted to showing how irrational and incoherent the various Gnostic systems are, and how they are frequently inconsistent with their own principles. Clement of Alexandria is very Hellenised in his background, and therefore instinctively sympathetic to the more intelligent Gnostics, but yet he remains implacably opposed to their views because he is clear on the authority of Scripture and on the transcendence of the Creator God who is also our redeemer. Men like these had enormous battles to fight, because they were swimming against the entire current of polytheistic, amoral, theosophical society. And we should honour them. They overcame. How did they do it? Essentially it was a battle over authority. Was it to be the authority of supposed secret revelations, or of the open records of Jesus and his disciples?

The sheer unity of the "great church" was a major factor that enabled it to stand firm against the various heresies, for it must be said that the different heretical systems hated each other as much as they hated the orthodox. Church unity had been a major feature in the apostolic writings, and it continued in their successors. Ignatius of Antioch, writing at the very start of the second century, insists that the local bishop is the focus of unity; without him the sacraments lacked efficacy and power.

A few years earlier, Clement of Rome had given what turned out to be even more important grounds for unity. He heard that the Corinthians had for no good reason rejected from church leadership orthodox people who stood in succession to the apostles, and he wrote to beg them to change their minds. This argument of succession from the apostles became a very valuable weapon, and bishops exploited it to the full. In contrast to the hidden secrets claimed by the differing Gnostic sects, the great church maintained an open recognition of the teachings of the apostles, safeguarded by their legitimate successors. This was impressive to the Gnostics and encouraging to the faithful. The original meaning of "apostolic succession" had no semi-magical connotations, but saw successive bishops in a see as guardians of the apostolic deposit in the Scriptures.

Second was their handling of Scripture. The different Gnostic sects either rejected the Old Testament entirely, like Marcion, or else made the Old Testament Scriptures mean what they wanted by the most fantastic allegorical interpretations. And although you find some of the church Fathers such as Irenaeus and Clement doing much the same at times, on the whole they took a fairly literal approach to the Scripture. They allowed it to speak to people on its own merits. And that was a powerful argument. They could show that their contemporary teaching was in line not only with the Old Testament but also with the "gospel and the apostle" as they called it, the gospel teaching about Jesus and the apostolic witness through their letters. It is very likely that the conflict with the Gnostics and with Marcion (and his narrow canon of an emasculated Gospel of Luke and the letters of Paul) stimulated the great church to accelerate the process already under way of regarding the teachings of the apostles "as the Lord himself".

A third factor which was obviously of value to the orthodox was their public acceptance of the Scriptures and the teachings of the apostles compared with the secret traditions to which the Gnostics laid claim. It looked a lot better and more credible to have open access to the origins of the faith than to paddle in the shadowlands of secret Gnostic speculation. Nobody ever read out the Gnostic material publicly in church. Nobody was nourished by it. And nobody met Jesus in it.

Naturally, the incipient canon was not known to all Christians, since its contents were limited in circulation by the lack of printing. So gradually the "rule of faith" became a very handy anti-Gnostic weapon. Men such as Irenaeus and Tertullian give this name to a short summary of the main truths of the gospel. Irenaeus declared that "the church, although scattered throughout the whole world ... has received the faith from the apostles and from their disciples. This is the faith in one God the Father Almighty, creator of heaven and earth and the seas and all that is in them, and in one Christ Jesus the Son of God, who was made flesh for our salvation, and in the Holy Spirit who through the prophets preached the saving plans and the coming of Christ, the virgin birth and the sufferings and resurrection from the dead, and the ascension into the heavens of our beloved Lord Jesus Christ in the flesh ... " Such summaries reflected the questions asked of candidates at baptism, and formed the nucleus of the later Apostles' Creed. They were very useful in giving the average Christian simple, clear answers to issues clouded in Gnostic speculation. They also had the advantage of giving firm rebuttal to Gnostic errors on God the Creator, the person of Christ, the nature of salvation, and the theme of promise and fulfilment linking the Old Testament with the New.

Finally, it seems clear that Christian lives outshone those of the Gnostics. There was a balance about their lives, an openness to inspection, a love for each other and those in need, and sheer practical goodness. Your average Gnostic was a solitary figure, rejoicing in being "one of a thousand or two of ten thousand". A favourite Gnostic text was "Blessed are the solitary and the chosen, for you will find the kingdom"! We do not hear of loving actions and generous deeds among the Gnostics. One is forced to ask what good (in practical terms) there was in knowing that "the archon who is weak has three names. The first name is Yalabaoth, the second is Saklas, and the third is Samael" (*Apocryphon of John*)! And that is the sort of thing the Gnostics loved.

So what's wrong with Gnosticism?

The Eastern Orthodox scholar Frederica Matthewes-Green has written with much insight on religious experiences and the debate between the Gnostics and the Christians. In her article "What heresy?", published in *Books and Culture*, 2003, she writes:

> Now you can begin to see what the early Christians found heretical.
>
> Gnosticism rejected the body and saw it as the prison for the soul: Christianity insisted that God infuses all his creation and that even the human body can be a vessel of holiness, a "temple of the holy Spirit".
>
> Gnosticism rejected the Hebrew Scriptures and portrayed the God of the Jews as an evil spirit: Christianity looked on Judaism as a mother.
>
> Gnosticism was elitist: Christianity was egalitarian, preferring "neither Jew nor Greek, male nor female, slave nor free".
>
> Finally Gnosticism was just too complicated. Christianity maintained the simple invitation of One who said "Let the little children come to me". Full-blown science-fiction Gnosticism died under its own weight.
>
> Let me put it another way.
>
> Authentic Christianity, as the great church steadfastly maintained, was rooted in the salvation achieved by the God who had created us – not salvation by any sort of esoteric knowledge.
>
> Authentic Christianity flowed from the honest and open gospel development of the divinely inspired Scriptures of the Old Testament – not from fantastic and secret theosophical speculations.

Authentic Christianity gets our reason to work on the revelation God has given in the Scriptures, rather than banishing reason and going for magical and irrational theosophy.

Authentic Christianity flows from a God who is both Creator and Redeemer and whose revelation is plain for all to see in both Old and New Testaments.

Authentic Christianity sees Jesus as the bridge between God and man – not countless archons and principalities with strange names.

Authentic Christianity demands a holy life of practical goodness, not the self-congratulation of an esoteric elite. It demands and empowers love both for brothers and sisters in the family of God and also for those who are not there yet – in contrast to the separatism and supercilious arrogance of the Gnostics.

Authentic Christianity does not hope, at the end of life, for some supposed divine spark, inherent in the elect, to be reunited with its source. It relies not on the salvation of those randomly predestined, but on the sheer generosity of God, whose free gift is eternal life for all who repent and believe.

Those are some of the things wrong with Gnosticism, and we can be thankful that, following the pioneering work of the New Testament writers, the church Fathers took such an unambiguous and militant stand against this dangerous heresy, elements of which are still around today, as we shall see in the chapters that follow.

Chapter Eleven

What Other Books Did the Church Reject?

Jt was not only the Gnostic gospels and "Acts" that the church denounced – and refused to have read in church – but other material which did not accord with those earliest testimonies to Jesus that came to form our New Testament. These fell into various categories.

Scattered Sayings

There are more than two hundred "agrapha", or unwritten sayings of Jesus, to be found scattered among the writings of the next few centuries. This reminds us that the gospel was something spoken long before it was written. And inevitably in the spoken word, changes get made and sources forgotten. Indeed, people with different viewpoints subtly twist the sayings of a famous person to suit their own opinions.

We find these purported sayings of Jesus beginning in the New Testament itself. In Acts 20:35, when Paul is saying farewell to the elders at the church in Ephesus, among whom he had worked so hard, he says, "Remember the words of the Lord Jesus, how he said, 'It is more blessed to give than to receive.'" Here is a saying that is so pure, so befitting the Jesus whom the Gospels present us with, that it is hard not to regard it as genuine. But we would never have known it had not Paul quoted it!

There is a fascinating example in what is known as the Western Text ("D") of St Luke's Gospel. It comes just after the pointed words of Jesus "The Son of man is Lord of the sabbath" (Luke 6:5) "D" then offers a short narrative which is complete in itself and thoroughly fits the context: "When on the same day he saw a man doing work on the sabbath, he said to him: 'Man, if you know what you are doing, you are blessed. But if you do not know it, you are accursed and a transgressor of the law.'" It may well be authentic.

As we saw in a previous chapter, there are sayings in the *Gospel of Thomas* that may well be original. The church Fathers, too, record such sayings as "If you ask for that which is great", Jesus says, "the small too will be added to you"; or "Ask for the heavenly, and you will also receive the earthly."

One of the most pungent second-century sayings purporting to come from Jesus is "Be good money-changers." Even Islam records several of these supposed sayings of Jesus, of which the most famous is written on a mosque in India: "The world is a bridge. Go over it – do not settle on it."

But, however well attested, the church set aside those sayings which claimed to come from Jesus that were not to be found in the New Testament records. The reason is clear. They knew the validity of the New Testament books, but they could not vouch for the authenticity of the scattered sayings. So they never even considered including them in the canon.

Novels

It may seem strange to think of early Christians writing novels. But they did! What else could you do? After all, the church did not encourage you to go to entertainments like gladiatorial shows, plays or exotic dances, and in some parts of the ancient world even school attendance was questionable, because of the violence and amorous liaisons of the pagan gods that figured largely in the curriculum. So what did they do with their long dark evenings? One answer is that they wrote romances. The late second-century *Clementine Recognitions* are splendid examples of these flights of fancy – harmless, orthodox stuff but entirely fictitious, with no historical value whatsoever.

Another example turned out to be rather more questionable. It is the *Acts of Paul and Thecla*, written quite early in the second century and attributed to the apostle Paul! It is great fun. St Paul appears not as an evangelist but as the advocate of sexual renunciation: only the chaste will be saved. In the city of Iconium one young woman, Thecla, becomes infatuated with his teaching and dumps her fiancé, Thanyris, who drags both her and Paul off to the magistrates. Paul escapes with a flogging, but she is condemned to death. As the flames shoot up around her, God sends a thunderstorm, and she escapes to follow Paul to Antioch, where another trial awaits her. The wealthy Alexander forces himself on her, is repulsed with ignominy, and Thecla is put on trial for assaulting one of the city's leading citizens! She is thrown to the lions, but a lioness comes and licks her feet, leaving Thecla alive and well. And so it goes on! A more serious assault by lions ensues, and eventually she jumps into a pool full of man-eating seals, crying out, "In the name of Jesus Christ, I am at last baptised." God intervenes again, a thunderbolt kills the seals, and Thecla emerges to preach the word of God back home in Iconium, where in the meantime her ex-fiancé has conveniently died!

All innocent enough stuff. Not a trace of Gnosticism in it. Nothing untoward except perhaps self-baptism by Thecla.

But no. The author of the book was sought out and arraigned. He turned out to be a presbyter who protested that his motives were as pure as driven snow: he had done it *amore Pauli*, out of love for Paul. But that did him no good. He was deposed from office. The church would have nothing to do with his work – though the fame of Thecla continued for centuries!

This story shows clearly that adding second-century stories to the New Testament was not tolerated even when New Testament places like Iconium and Antioch, and when New Testament names like Paul, Tryphaena and Alexander were invoked. The book was not part of the apostolic deposit. It was to be rejected.

Forgeries

As we have seen, a vast amount of the literature of the second century purports to be written by New Testament worthies – Philip, Thomas, Bartholomew, Mary, and so forth. And it is commonplace among theologians that this pseudepigraphy was regarded as a harmless little practice that was everywhere accepted. Nothing could be further from the truth. We have seen this in the case of *The Acts of Paul and Thecla*. But we can go much further back. St Paul's anger against the practice is evident when he heard that there had been a forgery of a letter in his name to the church at Thessalonica. "We beg you ... not to be quickly shaken in mind or excited, either by spirit or by word, or by *letter purporting to come from us*, to the effect that the day of the Lord has come" (2 Thessalonians 2:2). And he ends the letter pointedly, "I, Paul, write this greeting with my own hand. This is the mark in every letter of mine; it is the way I write" (2 Thessalonians 3:17). He had no time whatsoever for forgers. He did not regard it as a harmless little practice that everybody winked at.

Of course, many of the forgers liked to gain support by adducing a famous name for their own ideas. Others appended the name of a great man because they were too modest to put their own to the document – they did not consider themselves worthy. Others regarded themselves as giving a legitimate extension of their hero's views. Still others used the famous name to give credence to their heretical views. That seems to have been the situation with the *Gospel of Peter*. Eusebius tells us the story.

One of the better theologians towards the end of the second century was Serapion, Bishop of Antioch. One day he was visiting the tiny village of Rhossus, and found the Christians there using a gospel allegedly written by Simon Peter. It was entirely unknown to him, but he assumed it must be all right if it went out under such a famous name. So he got hold of a copy and took it home to Antioch with him. When he read it he realised that, though most of it was orthodox, some passages in it could be construed as docetic, denying the reality of our Lord's humanity. Part of the gospel has now been recovered (from the tomb of an eighth-century Egyptian monk!). Serapion was probably thinking of passages such as the unusual statement that when Jesus was being crucified "he was silent as if he had no pain", followed by the cry of dereliction "My power, my power, you have left me!" Serapion wrote a little pamphlet against it, *The So-called Gospel of Peter*, which surprisingly still survives today. In it he forbids any future use of the gospel. "For our part, brethren, we receive both Peter and the other apostles as Christ, but the writings which falsely bear their names we reject, as men of experience, knowing that such were not handed down to us" (Eusebius, *History of the Church*, 6:12). It was not so much its mildly docetic Christology and anti-Jewish stance that he found so offensive, but the fact that it was falsely attributed

to Peter, and was not handed down from earlier and forma-
tive generations of the church.

A recent find, which would certainly have drawn down
the wrath of the Fathers had they known of it, is the so-called
Secret Gospel of Mark. While he was cataloguing manuscripts
in the monastery of Mar Saba in the desert near Jerusalem in
1958, Professor Morton Smith came upon an amazing discovery. There was a spare page at the end of a seventeenth-century edition of the letters of Ignatius. This held a letter in
Greek, hitherto unknown, from Clement of Alexandria! It
quoted from a "mystic" gospel of Mark which was apparently
read in circles of initiates in Alexandria. The handwriting
itself came from the eighteenth century, but we are told that
it was a strange custom in that monastery to copy some part
of an ancient manuscript into the spare page or two at the
end of a book. In the letter Clement attacks the licentious
Carpocratians for distorting a "secret" gospel of our canonical Mark, written by the evangelist "for the use of those who
were attaining perfection", which Clement and his friends
read in Alexandria. So we are asked to believe there are three
Marks. One, the original Gospel in Rome. Two, the "spiritual"
or "mystic" version which appealed to Clement in Alexandria.
Three, the sexy Carpocration version of it. There we read that
a young man was raised from the dead by Jesus. "He looked at
Jesus, loved him, and asked to stay with him ... When it was
late the young man came to him, his naked body clothed only
with one linen garment, And he remained with him that
night; for Jesus was teaching him the mystery of the kingdom
of God."

Morton Smith has made the most of this, and incurred a
good deal of justified scepticism from his colleagues. He has
written it all up in scholarly monographs and in a popular
book, *Jesus the Magician*. He has suggested that Jesus was a

homosexual, and of course this has been manna from heaven for the film makers and scandalmongers. In addition, he suggests a magical baptismal ceremony. But there are massive question marks to raise over this document. Why is there no earlier attestation to this supposed letter of Clement? What is it doing in a printed eighteenth-century volume of Ignatius' letters? Why is it that no scholar apart from Smith has seen the original? Why is it that the original has disappeared? Was what the copyist wrote the copy of a genuine letter of Clement? Can we credit three versions of the Gospel of Mark circulating in Alexandria? Why is it that Clement never mentions the letter or the secret gospel, or the Carpocratians' corruption of it, in all his other writings? Morton Smith spent years on this letter and became infatuated with it. Some have even suggested that he forged it himself! Ancient texts copied over fifteen hundred years almost invariably exhibit textual errors, for copyists naturally made mistakes. Here there are none. What we have here looks not like a copy at all but like an original composition – forged either in the eighteenth century or the twentieth.

These are baffling questions to which we do not know the answers. What we can be sure about is that the church which accepted the Pauline strictures against immorality, and the Gospel picture of the purity of Jesus – the church, moreover, which roundly condemned the Carpocratians for their licentiousness – would never have given credence to this highly questionable "secret" account of Jesus and the young man. And, finally, there is a very interesting point. The last page of the volume of Ignatius' letters contains a stinging rebuke of those who forge documents. It concludes, "That very impudent fellow filled more pages with these trifles." And then follows the so-called letter of Clement! The inference is plain.

Finally we might glance at the so-called *Gospel of*

Barnabas. The Fathers would certainly have suppressed it had they known of it, but that was impossible since it was not written until the late Middle Ages, not earlier than the fourteenth century! Moreover, its earliest manuscripts are in Italian and Spanish! But it is often adduced by modern Muslim apologists as the one reliable *Injil* or gospel, of which our Gospels are corruptions. The book is sheer Muslim propaganda. It denies Jesus is the Son of God and makes him the forerunner who proclaims the future coming of Muhammad. It denies the crucifixion. It is packed with geographical and historical errors and breathes the atmosphere of the Middle Ages, not of the ancient East. The book contains some of the stories to be found in our Gospels, but with a strong Islamic slant. It is in fact a rather clumsy attempt to forge a life of Jesus that is consistent with Islamic beliefs, though it dares to contradict the Qur'an in various places. For instance it declares that Muhammad will be called the Messiah, though both the New Testament and the Qur'an give the title to Jesus alone. Again, in the Qur'an the birth of Jesus causes Mary pain, whereas in Barnabas it is said to be painless (a docetic twist, characteristic of Islamic Christology). The book is a worthless late forgery, and only deserves a mention because many modern Muslims use it in their propaganda. In all these areas we find the church declining to accept as norms for its beliefs and worship documents that do not come from the original core of the apostolic circle.

Chapter Twelve
Why Does All This Matter?

We have been considering the growth of the Christian collection of books, deemed crucial for its faith and life, during the first four centuries of the Christian era. But that is a very long time ago. It is all ancient history. What importance could it possibly have for our own day and generation?

Well, that is a good question, but there are at least four compelling answers to it.

All this matters for the sake of integrity

In the past one would have said "It matters for the sake of truth," but in our day, when truth is often dismissed as a power game, that would take us far afield from our topic. Let us say that it matters for the sake of integrity, sheer honesty, which even in these days of the deconstructing of all virtues still remains broadly desirable. And in books such as Dan Brown's *The Da Vinci Code* and similar novels, or even academic studies that rely on the Gnostic gospels, there is a plain lack of integrity on the part of their authors.

Take Dan Brown as a best-selling example. At the outset of his novel he has a page entitled "Fact". In it he makes several dubious claims and then concludes, "All descriptions of artwork, architecture, documents and secret rituals in this novel are accurate." They are not. Numerous critics have pointed out the glaring errors in the book, but Brown refuses to debate them. He sits back, ignores the criticisms and rakes in the cash. The main thrust of his contention is that Jesus survived crucifixion, married Mary Magdalene, had a child with her and established a dynasty whose survivors are still around in France today. There is not a word of truth in this, but if it sounds a bit familiar, you have only to go to a best-seller back in the 1980s to find it. It is *The Holy Blood and The Holy Grail*, produced by Michael Baigent, Richard Leigh and Harry Lincoln. The plot is suspiciously similar. Men like this trio and their successor Brown inevitably find problems with the Gospels! So they manipulate, explain away or distort the evidence they find there. This is unbelievably bad scholarship, even for a novel. To reject the testimony of those who lived alongside Jesus, in favour of fourth-century Coptic Gospels found in a rubbish heap in the Egyptian sands is astonishingly wrong-headed. To claim that Constantine, the first Christian Emperor, destroyed thousands of original manuscripts that told the story of a merely human Jesus is sheer fantasy. The claim is entirely without foundation. He destroyed no manuscripts; but we do possess a great many manuscripts written long before Constantine and coming from every quarter of the then known world, and none of them betray substantive editorial changes. Apart from scribal errors, the text of the New Testament is rock solid.

As for the suggestion that you get a merely human Jesus in the Gospels, it is ridiculous. The divinity as well as humanity of Jesus is there for all to see. In Matthew's preface Jesus is "Emmanuel" (God with us) and "Jesus" (God to the rescue). Mark's opening words are "The beginning of the gospel of Jesus Christ, the Son of God". Luke's first chapter records "He shall be called the Son of God," while the fourth Gospel has a marvellous prelude about the Word actually being God and being flesh, and concludes it with these words: "No one has ever seen God; it is God the only Son, who is close to the Father's heart, who has made him known" (John 1:18). Brown must know this, but he deliberately turns his back on it in pursuance of his story, and tells us the laughable untruth that Jesus was only deified at the council of Nicaea so that the pagan (!) Constantine could consolidate his power base. That sort of writing might be all right in sheer fiction, but Brown claims it as solid fact. The latter may be thought more probable.

Another example of Brown's embarrassing confusions is this. He claims that the Gnostic gospels, which he loves, were excluded from the Bible because they speak of Christ's ministry in very human terms. But that is rubbish. Our Gospels have lots about the human life and ministry of Jesus, but the Gnostic gospels have almost nothing. They were never even considered for the Christian canon, and are largely collections of bizarre secret sayings by a divine Jesus who only appears to be human. Brown ignores this evidence.

Again, his claim that our Gospels only became authoritative in the fourth century, and that they were chosen from among 80 gospels vying for inclusion in the canon, is laughable, as we have seen above. The four Gospels, and they alone, were recognised as supremely reliable testimonies to Jesus from the very start.

Brown maintains that the Dead Sea Scrolls and the Gnostic gospels, found respectively in 1947–56 and in 1945 (he gets the dates wrong!), are the earliest Christian records. However, in fact the Dead Sea Scrolls say nothing at all about Jesus because they were written well before his birth, while the Gnostic gospels were written long after our Gospels! Far from it being the case, as Teabing, Brown's protagonist, maintains, that "almost everything our fathers taught us about Christ is false," in point of fact almost everything Brown says about Jesus is false.

He has, of course, his own agenda. He wants to make Jesus the original feminist, who celebrated the eternal feminine which is central to the paganism Brown regards as superior to Christianity. He is also keen to discredit the Vatican, as were his predecessors Baigent, Leigh and Lincoln in their book *The Dead Sea Scrolls Deception*, and so commits many palpable errors, such as that the Catholic Church tried desperately to prevent the publication of these Coptic scrolls. In fact they did not even have access to them during the decisive years after their discovery! It says something about the credulity of our enlightened age that such a book, full of such inaccuracies and distortions while claiming absolute truth, should become a best-seller!

But unfortunately the question of distortion must also be raised against the academics who favour this revisionist line – Morton Smith with his idea that he has found a page from some early version of Mark which makes Jesus out to be a homosexual and a magician, or Elaine Pagels and Karen King with their claim that there was no clear concept of orthodoxy in the church until the fourth century. We have had occasion to take issue with these scholars in the body of the book, but here it is worth pointing out that Pagels knows that the vast majority of scholars insist that the *Gospel of Thomas* is secondary to our Gospels. She knows perfectly well that men such as Irenaeus and Tertullian were passionate for orthodoxy and were very clear about the "rule of faith" and the unique authority of the apostolic material. When the Muratorian Canon (which she does not mention) refuses to receive "the heresy of Marcion and several others which cannot be received into the catholic church, for it is not fitting to mix poison with honey", is it not obvious that there is a clear concept of orthodoxy? And although in her book *The Gnostic Gospels* she denies taking sides with the Gnostics, her true position becomes very plain in her later book *Beyond Belief*, where she chronicles her rejection of orthodoxy and her journey towards a reconfigured variation on Christianity: self-actualisation. For her, as for Gnostic thought, "theology is a matter of anthropology," as she puts it. Pagels does not write as an impartial scholar. Her study of Gnosticism coincides with her own spiritual journey and encourages her to postulate a widespread authority for these Gnostic tests, and then to suggest that the canonisation of the New Testament documents was arbitrary. This is not disinterested scholarship!

Karen King, author of *The Gospel of Mary of Magdala: Jesus and the First Woman Apostle*, is not only imposing a markedly feminist agenda on the material (the church suppressed the true role of Mary of Magdala as the first woman apostle, and turned her into a whore!) but is unjustifiably claiming that the norm of early Christianity was theological diversity not consensus. To be sure, there is plenty of diversity to be found in the pages of the New Testament and the stances of its authors, but that is a very different matter from arguing that Gnostic material circulated in Christian circles with parallel credentials. As we have seen, it did not. The church rejected Gnosticism wholeheartedly and continuously from the first century onwards, and a scholar of the erudition of Karen King must surely know it.

The Gnostic gospels never came near being considered for inclusion in the canon, even in Egypt where many of them originated. It simply is not the case that the fourth-century church deleted them in favour of our four Gospels.

So it seems to me that the examination of books like *The Da Vinci Code* and the academic patrons whose work undergirds it is important because they raise in very sharp focus

the question of truth and integrity. Without them our civilisation is heading for disaster.

All this matters for the sake of society

It is not just personal integrity that is at stake in the massive
adulation that has been poured upon this brilliantly conceived but flawed book, *The Da Vinci Code*. These issues matter
because of the sort of society we are becoming.

In December 2004 a poll on religious views was held in
Britain. If it can be relied on, it shows that there has been a
massive decline in religious belief in the past 20 years. Few
would deny it. Nowadays a mere 44% of people profess to
believe in God, and it is by no means only the monotheistic
God of the Judaeo-Christian faith that they believe in; it may
be some vague Life Force, some inscrutable Superior Being,
the pagan Gaia or even themselves. Marriage is no longer
seen as a sacrament or as preferably permanent, and a majority of young people would not want to be married in church.
The beliefs that have moulded much of art and culture, such
as faith in life after death, in heaven, hell and the devil, are all
now decidedly minority views. There is as yet little overt
opposition to religion in Britain. Most Brits are simply apa-
thetic: persecution may well come later.

That would be true for many countries in Europe. Indeed,
there are only a couple of countries within the European
Union where Christians are still a majority: Poland and
Ireland. Elsewhere, secularism is the prevailing world view,
although God keeps popping up unexpectedly when a
Princess Diana or a Pope John Paul dies, or in the aftermath
of 9/11. But the effects of such religious spurts are short-lived.
Much of European culture lacks any firm beliefs, other than

doing our own thing, not harming other people, and enjoying our own pleasures. The question is, does this matter?

Yes it does. Because those who, like Arnold Toynbee, have studied the history of civilisations are agreed on this: where there is no energising faith, civilisations crumble. Every civilisation that has ceased to be inspired by the vision and values that once sprang from the faith at its core has not lasted for very long.

The writer Os Guinness has recently made some very pertinent observations on this point, and I am much indebted to him. He points out that Western civilisation has been built very largely on the Christian faith. Our universities, hospitals, science and human rights all derive largely from a Christian basis. Can they survive its demise? The omens are not propitious. For there is, he argues, an unbreakable link between faith and freedom, for the simple reason that faith requires an ultimate belief system: without it there are no roots to the rights by which freedom flourishes. Dr Guinness suggests a triangle. Freedom requires virtue. Virtue requires faith. Faith requires freedom. But as we look around us we see virtue widely discounted, morality arbitrary, and crime escalating. A "Look after No. 1" attitude pervades. Virtue requires faith, but today there is little faith and only tattered remains of virtue. Faith still has some freedom, but that is being increasingly inhibited by the banishing of Christian teaching from schools, the requirements of political correctness, and legislation making negative comment about other faiths a crime punishable by a prison sentence.

These seem to be some of the fruits of our departure from the Judaeo-Christian faith of our forebears and towards the Gnostic view of ourselves as the source of our salvation, and our esoteric knowledge as the key to personal and societal fulfilment. We must never forget that the Gnostics were essentially selfish and individualistic. They never made successful societies because they were taken up with their own fortunes and did not bother about others. Our society is slipping dangerously in that direction. And the move from a faith based in a historic Saviour from beyond ourselves, to one based entirely on our own inner resources, is very evident in the "self-help" strategies so common today. It is a very dangerous shift. The issues examined in this book are part at least of this undeniable change of direction in public and private life. That is why they matter for society.

All this matters for the sake of the church

Moreover, the matters discussed in this book are highly germane to the future of the church. If the revisionist views of the likes of Professors King and Pagels prevail, the church will collapse, just as the Gnostics did. Indeed, the process is well on the way. It may seem very strange to suggest that Gnosticism is still alive and well in Christian circles. But such is undoubtedly the case.

The discovery of the Gnostic texts at Nag Hammadi has produced a lively new interest in Gnosticism, and this has influenced both the arcane sphere of New Testament studies and the practical life of the churches.

On the New Testament front, the more mythological forms of Gnosticism have given fresh impetus to contemporary theosophical speculation and various occult groups. But much more important is the impact of Gnosticism on the so-called Jesus Seminar, founded by Robert Funk, and comprising, besides a few serious scholars, a variety of writers on the fringe of New Testament studies who hold extreme, indeed bizarre views.

Their method of proceeding is well known. As we saw in

Chapter One, they examine each of the sayings of Jesus and attempt to assess its authenticity by throwing different coloured marbles into a bowl, according to whether they regard the saying as authentic to Jesus, a product of the church, or indeterminate. This is of course an outrageous procedure, and most New Testament scholars will have nothing to do with it. But the extreme nature of their conclusions and the skill of their publicity mean that they get noticed. In any event, you will find among the members of the Seminar a high regard for the *Gospel of Thomas*, which some of them try to date before the four Gospels. This enables them to maintain many tenets that come straight from the ancient Gnostics, notably a docetic Christology which drives a massive wedge between the Jesus of history and the Christ of faith, and a redefinition of the nature of God. For them, whatever God there might be has certainly not revealed himself in Jesus of Nazareth!

For example, Marcus Borg, lately Professor of Religion at Oregon State University, maintains (quite wrongly) that orthodox Christianity sees only the transcendence of the God who is "out there" and does not make room for the God who is immanent in the world. Consequently, "experience" is his buzzword, and he argues for Panentheism, the semi-Gnostic view that the universe is part of God and emanated from the Creator, in contrast to the Christian view that God is transcendent over his created world but is also immanent within it and cares for it. Panentheism can lead both to the worship of nature and to the worship of ourselves, and there is plenty of evidence of both in today's society with its cult of Gaia and idealisation of human potential. The Gnostic roots are unmistakable.

It is much the same with the tendency of other Jesus Seminar members to postulate a docetic Christology. Rudolf

Bultmann led the way, but many of his followers, including Paul Achtemeier, maintain that we must not place faith in any supposed historical events but in the proclamation of the word. This looks impressive, but it is nothing of the sort. It means that we cannot or need not believe in the historical resurrection of Jesus from the dead, for it is impossible to demonstrate and is in any case irrelevant. You see, if the body is the prison of the divine soul, then what matters is not some supposed historical event but our inner illumination, our spiritual vision – not literal seeing. These scholars (who cannot begin to contend with the evidence marshalled in N.T. Wright's magisterial book *The Resurrection of the Son of God*) set out to advocate the essentially Gnostic position that the appearances of Jesus after his death were "inner revelatory experiences" and it was these experiences that led the disciples to proclaim that Jesus rose from the dead. Inner illumination, divorced from history, is precisely what the Gnostics were all about. When you ground your faith not in history but in inner experience there is no check on it. It can run wild, as it does when James M. Robinson of Claremont University tells us that we need a Christology that will meet our conditions, and then offers us a wedding of Sophia to Jesus in a chapter entitled "Very Goddess and Very Man". Sea Raven informs us in her book *Jesus is our Sophia: The Historical Jesus and the Cosmic Christ* that "Jesus and Sophia are manifestations of the cosmic Christ" and "The man Jesus, the pre-Easter Jesus, was not the Christ. Jesus became the Christ or was revealed as the Christ after his death." This is pure Gnosticism – a mixture of adoptionism and the authority of inner revelations unchecked by historical events.

But it is not only in the Jesus Seminar that strong Gnostic influences are alive and well. We have already seen in earlier chapters that Professors King and Pagels are eloquent advocates of a position that has two interlocking aspects. One is that early Christianity had no idea of heresy, but that a whole variety of mutually contradictory versions of Christianity flourished alongside each other, and only became differentiated as orthodoxy and heresy in the fourth century – a view which is, as we have seen, quite at odds with the evidence. They also maintain that women, particularly Mary Magdalene, had a leading position in these circles and a significance much greater than that of the original male disciples because of the inner illumination that Jesus had elicited in them. The *Gospel of Philip* and the *Gospel of Mary*, the books which (among others of the same character) the church suppressed, are the fourth-century Gnostic sources from which these views come! As we have seen, Elaine Pagels explicitly acknowledges as much. She tells us how the saying (no. 70) in the *Gospel of Thomas*, itself quintessentially Gnostic – "If you bring forth what is within you, what you bring forth will save you" – seemed to her self-evidently true, for it does not tell us what to believe (that she cannot stand!) but to discover what lies hidden within ourselves. That is high-grade Gnosticism, which would have gone down wonderfully well in second-century Gnostic circles. The Gnostic appealed to the deified self and personal internal experiences as the final authority in religion. Catholic orthodoxy relied on the solid evidence of the historical Jesus, and apostolic testimony to him. The battle was on in the second century. It is on again today.

If this is the continuing effect of Gnosticism in academia, it is not surprising that it has affected the church. And nowhere is this more evident than in the Episcopal Church of the United States, where we can see it clearly and in a well developed form. This wealthy church, though numbering fewer than a couple of million, has been highly significant in American society. Many presidents of the United States have been members of it. It was part of the mainstream Trinitarian Christianity which has been the norm for many centuries. But now all that is changing. For the past 30 years and more that Church has been systematically moving away from its biblical moorings. At its last General Convention in 2004 it repudiated the ultimate authority of the Bible, and many of its bishops declare that "it was the church that gave us the Bible in the first place. The church can rewrite it." Moreover, that same Convention confirmed the election of a man as bishop who had divorced his wife, abandoned his family and daughters, and was now living brazenly in homosexual union with a male partner. Both in faith and morals the Episcopal Church had abandoned the "faith once for all delivered to the saints". They were led by a skilled diplomat who operated on the principle of the pluriformity of truth, which enabled him to change sides at the flick of a switch. This was very evident when, in October 2003, the Archbishop of Canterbury called an extraordinary meeting of the Primates (leaders of the various Anglican Provinces in the world) to discuss the crisis that would emerge if this consecration were to take place. They agreed that it would tear apart the fabric of the Communion. The Presiding Bishop shared in the unanimous rebuttal of this prospective consecration, and then he went straight back to the States and presided at it! He adopts the typical "Alice in Wonderland" method of making words mean what he wants them to mean. In addition he displays a typically Gnostic reliance on inner illumination whether or not it hurts other people (it threw the worldwide Anglican Communion into turmoil) or relates at all to historic Christianity.

One of my friends, a distinguished Episcopal leader in the States, has made considerable study of the results of this Gnostic departure from the historic documents of Christianity in the direction of a higher knowledge of inner illumination. He develops the argument of Harold Bloom, in *The American Religion* (1992), that the civic belief system of America is not Protestant Christianity at all, but a form of Gnosticism which regards the True Self as the source of all spiritual authority. Canon Filmore Strunk fleshes this out ably and provocatively in his evaluation of the Episcopal Church. He points out the mass of contrasts between orthodox Christianity and the "Modern Gnosticism" which he sees, with good reason, as characterising the contemporary Episcopal Church of the United States of America. I include some of his contrasts in column form.

A comparison of modern Gnosticism and orthodox Christianity

The Issues	Modern Gnosticism	Orthodox Christianity
Core Proclamation	You have an inner spark of the divine, an inner light coeternal with God. Spiritual knowledge (gnosis) lets it shine.	"For God so loved the world that he gave his one and only Son [Jesus Christ] that whoever believes in him shall not perish, but have eternal life." (John 3:16)
Revelation originates ...	from within – the True Self.	from without – God.
The heart (the emotive function) is ...	the source of all truth. Trust it entirely.	"deceitful above all things ... who can understand it?" (Jeremiah 17:9)
The Bible is ...	like other religious texts, a literary creation of its human authors. It contains some useful metaphors, but also reflects the patriarchal, benighted values of an unenlightened age.	the creation of the Holy Spirit, working through various human authors, authoritative in its teachings, reflecting the timeless will of God for all humanity.
Attitude toward the Biblical mandates	Suspicion	Trust

The Issues	Modern Gnosticism	Orthodox Christianity
Attitude toward the cultural mandates	Trust	Suspicion
Human beings are ...	innately good, rightly reserving judgment on all truth claims in the light of the highest value – unfettered personal choice.	sinful and needing a saviour, yet loved and pursued by God; able to choose God and the new life God brings by his grace alone.
The doctrine of original sin is ...	a destructive belief designed by ancient power elites as a tool to suppress individuality, creativity and self-esteem.	the most objectively discernable Christian doctrine, given by God to show us our need of Christ's redeeming work.
Jesus of Nazareth is ...	a shadowy figure who may have lived in the first century CE, and who may have taught a message of love and acceptance.	God in the flesh, who healed the sick, cast out demons, performed miracles and taught a message of love, repentance and transformation.
The passion of Christ is ...	a nonsensical, disgusting description of child abuse. What loving father would send a son to be killed?	Jesus offering himself for our sins, gaining victory over sin and death. It is proof of God's love.
Our greatest quest	Loving the True Self and creating a life path.	Loving God and keeping God's commandments.
Marriage is ...	a patriarchal, oppressive relic of a practice depicting men's ownership of women. It must be radically redefined to fit today's cultural norms.	instituted by God. It is the sacramental embodiment of Christ's love for his church embodied in the permanent, covenantal intimacy of a man and a woman.
Sex outside marriage ...	is nobody's business but your own. It asserts unfettered choice, and is, therefore, sacred.	is sin. It mocks the permanent, covenantal, life-creating love of Christ.
Attitude towards the body	Your body belongs to you. Use it as you will. Anybody who tries to tell you to use your body in a way you do not want is simply attempting to oppress you and stifle your innate individuality.	"Do you not know that your body is a temple of the Holy Spirit, who is in you, whom you have received from God? You are not your own; you were bought with a price. Therefore honour God with your body." (1 Corinthians 6:19c–20)

The Issues	Modern Gnosticism	Orthodox Christianity
Biblical language proscribing homosexual behaviour is ...	hate-speech.	a gift from God, which, if followed, would have resulted in thousands of lives being saved, and untold suffering averted.
Homosexuals are ...	an oppressed minority who must be liberated from the hateful prejudice of orthodox Christians. Since they are icons of personal choice, they are sacred.	like everybody else, loved by God just as they are, and deserving right treatment. Like everybody else, they are called to turn from destruction to obedient life.

Source: Filmore Strunk. Used by permission.

Not everyone will agree with every detail outlined on the following pages; but the general direction is undeniable. Here is a prestigious modern Church, in the most important country in the world, which has been extensively penetrated by Gnosticism. It is the most glaring example among contemporary Christian churches, but other churches are moving in the same direction. Let it be clearly understood that this is the direction taken by Gnosticism, which the Fathers of the undivided church so fervently sought to suppress. And let it be equally clearly understood that this is a very long way from historic Christianity.

Yes, all this does matter – for the sake of honest handling of historical sources, for the sake of our culture and for the sake of the church.

It matters for the sake of the individual

There is no doubt that the approach of Brown in his book is wildly popular. There are many reasons for this. A non-authoritarian age rather admires these Gnostic rebels against the church establishment. A libertarian age likes the permissiveness that paganism offers. An independent age hates being told what to believe. The hunger for spirituality (but aversion to Christianity) makes modern Gnosticism an attractive alternative. The feminism that is there in Pagels and King, but absent in the ancient texts, has a big appeal these days. The cult of the "sacred feminine", with its worship of nature and full sexual permissiveness, is very attractive in a hedonistic age that is losing touch with the transcendent and seeing this world as all there is. It even suggests the way to a universal naturalistic religion replacing the established religions. So there is no shortage of reasons for its appeal. But all the same it is poison.

For we must never forget that it is not merely integrity, the future of society, and the corruption of the church that are being affected by all this Gnostic revisionism, but real human beings. And therein lies no small part of its tragedy. For ordinary men and women are being led astray. They know so little of the gospel truths these days that they are easily beguiled. As G.K. Chesterton observed: "When men give up belief in God, they do not believe in nothing – they believe in anything." And that is what is happening as thousands upon thousands feast on books like Brown's. They are being encouraged to believe that sin is merely a man-made concept. They are encouraged not to regard Jesus as the Son of God. They are encouraged to believe that what they know will save them. They are encouraged to believe that what comes from their own inner resources will suffice to rescue them from all problems in this life and the next.

But this is sheer delusion. If our own unaided effort had sufficed, Jesus would never have come to this world for us. If we were adequate to transform our lives into what they should be, he could have saved himself the effort. If we really were divine this world would not be in the mess it is! The tragedy of books like *The Da Vinci Code* is not so much their error as their persuasiveness. Men and women are being lured into believing a lie, the ancient Gnostic lie which the early church fought so tenaciously to suppress. Brown is offering men and women a spirituality that does not work. He is proffering sex and "the Force" instead of relationship with a transcendent Lord. And so people are being sold a lie that will never provide the satisfaction for which they hunger and thirst. That is why all this matters so much.

Chapter Thirteen

The "Sacred Feminine" - Where Is It Leading Us?

We have concentrated throughout this book on the question of how reliable are the Gnostic gospels which underlie the various attempts at revisionism that we have had reason to examine. Our conclusion is unambiguous. These documents are unreliable, late, and destructive of Christianity. But interwoven with the unfounded claims about the Gnostic gospels is a constant theme celebrating the "sacred feminine". This occurs both in a novel such as *The Da Vinci Code* and in some scholarly works, notably those by Karen King and Elaine Pagels. What lies behind this new fascination with the "sacred feminine"? Is it merely an expression of our contemporary pan-sexuality? Or radical feminism? Or is it, perhaps, advancing a world view in strong contradistinction to Christianity?

Let us begin by looking at the place feminism and sexuality in general play in Brown's book *The Da Vinci Code*.

There is plenty about sex in this book, but it is not a sex book. As is well known, the sub-plot of the book is that Jesus had a child by his wife, Mary Magdalene, whose descendants through the feminine line are still around. One of them is Sophie, the beautiful redheaded cryptographer, and her name seems to suggest the *Sophia* (Wisdom) so popular among the Gnostics. This secret bloodline, we are told, was ruthlessly suppressed by Christ's male apostles and by the Fathers of the church. Brown asserts that apocryphal gospels which give Mary Magdalene her due were excluded from the New Testament by order of Constantine; and Mary, the "divine feminine", was demonised as a prostitute. A small part of Brown's agenda is to restore her to the primacy in the church that he argues Christ intended her to have, over against the male apostles.

It is ironic that Brown should turn to the Gnostic gospels in order to support this farrago of nonsense, which has been scorned by every competent reviewer of his book. The fact is that the Gnostics were very opposed to the feminine. They did not even approve of women giving birth, because that was to entomb yet other sparks of divinity within human bodies, which they regarded as hopelessly corrupt. The ideal Gnostic model is either a male or an androgynous being complete in itself. Women never had any leadership role in Gnostic circles. But perhaps Brown does not know that! Even a dedicated feminist like Karen King observes, "It seems to me that even when the feminine is highly valued, it is often done so at the expense of real sexuality. It also seems as though gnostic mythology and gender imagery often affirm patriarchy and patriarchal social gender roles."

But the glorification of Mary Magdalene and female leadership hardly touches the heart of the book's approach to sexuality. Brown asserts that the act of sex is where you find "divinity", and that the church through the ages recast sex between men and women as a shameful act, in order to combat a threat to the base of its power. It is true that the attitude to sex has been prudish if not worse among a number of Christian theologians down the ages. However, that is certainly not the attitude of the Bible, which celebrates sex as one of God's very best gifts to humankind. The Old Testament maintains that the one-flesh relationship between man and wife is fundamental to God's purpose (Genesis 2:24). It tells of Isaac fondling his wife in Genesis 26:8, of explicit sexual enjoyment in Proverbs 5:18ff, and the Song of Songs is a love poem full of erotic imagery. The New Testament celebrates the marriage bed as pure (Hebrews 13:4) and in Ephesians 5 even makes the man-woman relationship parallel to that between Christ and the church! So, while it is true that the Bible is against all forms of sexual expression outside marriage, it is positively enthusiastic about the joy and fulfilment found within marriage. To be sure, many of the church Fathers were unduly restrictive in their attitudes because of the gross and unrestrained sexual chaos all around them, and because they regarded virginity and martyrdom as two of the costliest ways in which a person could show their loyalty to Jesus. But the Bible itself celebrates sexuality, and maintains that people are not separated by culture, social status, education or gender but by whether or not they are committed to Christ. Galatians 3:28 is a seminal expression of this liberated attitude to women as well as men: "There is no longer Jew or Greek, there is no longer slave or free, there is no longer male or female; for all of you are one in Christ Jesus."

We get nearer to the essence of Brown's position in the most graphic scene in the book. It is what Brown calls the *hieros gamos*, the "sacred marriage", where masked men and women engage in a sexual orgy. His hero explains that this is not really about eroticism but rather a very ancient ceremony designed by the ancient Egyptians to promote fertility. It was here that the participants encountered the god. The man could achieve knowledge of the divine through orgasm, and the woman through the miracle of childbearing. He says, "The ability of the woman to produce life from her womb made her sacred. A god." This age-old ceremony of sacred marriage points to the only communion with the divine we shall ever experience. "The next time you find yourself with a woman, look in your heart and see if you cannot approach sex as a mystical, spiritual act. Challenge yourself to find that spark of divinity that man can only achieve through the sacred feminine." "The women smiled knowingly, nodding," he adds, while "the men exchanged dubious giggles and off-colour jokes." It is the women who understand.

The *Gospel of Philip* hints broadly at all this. It has a lot to say about the "bridal chamber", which was reserved for the private initiations of "free men and virgins". According to Irenaeus, mantras were sung in the ceremony until the man could achieve a climactic instant when his mind went blank and he could see God. That is the sort of sex that Brown advocates – a physical union for spiritual ecstasy. It is through this that we can attain "altered consciousness", an ecstatic mindless experience. This has of course got close connections with Eastern spirituality. In Hindu and Buddhist meditation the prime aim of spiritual ecstasy (to which not just orgasm but profound meditation is another route) is often achieved through the constant repetition of a mantra until the mind goes blank. In other words, as New Age gurus maintain, the enemy of meditation is the mind. And that is precisely the position advocated by the ancient Gnostics. The *Tripartite Tractate* encourages readers to be "filled with the Spirit but be emptied of reason". What a contrast that is to a Christianity that sees the mind as one of the greatest marks of the image of God in humankind.

The plot thickens as we examine the concept of androgyny, the fusing of male and female. In the scene Brown paints of the *hieros gamos*, all are wearing masks, the men black and the women white. The Mona Lisa is smiling, because that name really conceals Amon and L'Isa (Isis), the androgynous pair, also represented by the androgynous figure next to Jesus at Leonardo's Last Supper. Both paintings, Brown believes, present an image that is neither male nor female but a subtle combination of the two. The Mona Lisa smiles because she knows this. She has *gnosis*. This means, of course, that we can equally celebrate homosexuality and heterosexuality. Indeed it even makes any form of sexual expression normal. If sex is the route to spirituality, the more the merrier ... of any kind of sex.

Does this matter, apart from the vexed question of the propriety of homosexual acts? Yes it does. Because the joining of opposites means that those joined in this way rise above all distinctions, which, as the Hindus say, are mere illusion, *maya*. And if that is the case, where is the difference between good and evil? There is none. The Gnostic text *Thunder, Perfect Mind*, much loved by Elaine Pagels, makes this very clear. A woman who claims to be Isis says, with an all-inclusiveness that resonates with today's political correctness, "I am the whore and the holy one, the wife and the virgin, knowledge and ignorance, shame and shamelessness. I am sinless and the root of sin derives from me. I am the one called truth and iniquity." Here is a claim to spirituality that transcends the difference between right and wrong, and regards them equally. This is the direction in which Brown is wanting to lead us, and millions of people are being carried along by the story and duped by his world view, which fits so comfortably with twenty-first-century "totalitolerance" and hedonism.

We must not fail to notice where this claim to transcend the difference between right and wrong leads: straight to the contention of one of the figures in the book that "it was *man*, not God, who created the concept of ... sin." If you can transcend the difference between right and wrong, you eradicate the concept of sin and guilt – and equally, therefore, of redemption. This is classic Gnosticism, and indeed sits well with the pagan Mystery Religions, which purported to offer the initiates salvation. For that is what Gnosticism has done: it has transformed Christianity into one of the mystery cults that were so popular in the ancient world. In Gnosticism, as in the Mysteries, you were saved by knowledge, not by Christ. And that is why the Gnostic gospels have nothing to say about the history of Jesus, and nothing about his death and resurrection, the core of Christian salvation. The cross and resurrection are alien to the Gnostic world view of theosophy and arrogance.

But it is when we come to what the book says about the Goddess that we penetrate to the centre of what Brown is doing. He made it very clear in a talk show on ABC 20/20 on American TV that he is concerned to supplant Christianity by a thinly disguised return to paganism. The church "demonised the sacred feminine, obliterating the goddess from modern religion for ever", and Brown intends to reverse all that. The Goddess represents age-old worship of Nature. Ishtar, Cybele, Asherah, Aphrodite, Isis – all different names in different cultures for the worship of the feminine principle which gives life to all and bridges the way into the unseen world. As Peter Jones observes in his book *Cracking Da Vinci's Code*, co-authored with James Carlow, "the title of a book written a few years ago expresses *The Da Vinci Code*'s deep message: *The Once and Future Goddess: A Symbol for our Time*." He observes, correctly, that "the sacred feminine really means the reign of Mother Nature ... The sacred feminine assures us that everything in Nature, including our inner self, is divine." It is a return to pre-Christian pagan Pantheism.

This is proving attractive to many in this New Age of Aquarius who are glad to see the libertarian pre-Christian Goddess replacing the God of the Bible. Within less than a generation we have seen a massive departure from the Age of Pisces, when the fish which represented Christianity was in the ascendant. There are new and radical views of the family, sexuality, gender roles, education, morals, marriage and God on offer these days. *The Da Vinci Code* has expressed to the many the ideals of the few, and has done so in an explosive novel and film. We are being offered a radical alternative to the Christian faith and the values it embodies. Old Nature worship advances towards us in a new dress with full sexual permissiveness, and the blending of opposing religions and philosophies into a single syncretistic system. It bids fair to become a single world religion uniting all faiths under Nature and the Goddess. Like a mediaeval troubadour, Brown has issued an ideological call to arms.

But of course he does not stand alone. As we have seen earlier in the book there is not only the Jesus Seminar in the background behind him, but also two women professors, Elaine Pagels and Karen King, together with less distinguished writers who adopt a similar position.

Karen King's *The Gospel of Mary of Magdala: Jesus and the First Woman Apostle* is written from a strongly feminist perspective. She believes that the official church documents have grossly underestimated the role of women in the unfolding history of the church. Their work has been almost completely submerged in deference to the control of their male colleagues. She argues, "The male Jesus selects male disciples who pass on tradition to male bishops. Yet we know that in the early centuries and throughout Christian history women played prominent roles as apostles, teachers, preachers and prophets." She maintains, moreover, that there were multiple models and widely divergent versions of Christianity in the early days, and that such words as heresy and orthodoxy are out of place until the fourth century. Amazingly, she even dares to declare that "the invention of Gnosticism and Jewish Christianity" belongs not to the first centuries but to modern scholars!

Now that will not do at all. We have seen in an earlier chapter that whereas Mary Magdalene could properly be said, as Hippolytus recognised, to have been "an apostle to the apostles", in that she was the one to announce the resurrection to them, there is not a shred of evidence that she or any other woman was given any official position in the church, let alone as an apostle of Jesus Christ in the same sense that the Twelve and Paul were. Not a shred! There were indeed a few women teachers in the church, such as Priscilla (Acts 18:26), but she worked with her husband, Aquila; or Thecla in the second century, but her behaviour was regarded by many as scandalous. There were indeed some prophetesses, notably the prophesying daughters of Philip of whom we read in Acts and who were famous in the second century. But women prophets fell into sharp decline after the excesses of Maximilla and Prisca, the companions of the heretic Montanus. King's view that the early church cheerfully held together a wide spectrum of views, including those represented in the Gnostic gospels, has not one iota of support. It is entirely an argument from silence, and it is shot to pieces by the powerful attacks from Christian writers such as Justin, Irenaeus and Tertullian in the second century on these Gnostic views which were so obviously at variance with the deposit of the apostles to be found in our Gospels. These church Fathers would have been flabbergasted to be told that Gnosticism and Jewish Christianity were creations of modern scholars!

It is a pity that King makes no reference to Martin Hengel, *The Four Gospels and the One Gospel of Jesus Christ*, or to J.D.G. Dunn, *Unity and Diversity in the New Testament*. They would have saved her some serious mistakes, particularly the notion that there was a whole variety of different forms of Christianity, divergent and mutually contradictory, floating around in the early church, and happily accepted by its leaders! Indeed, had she turned her attention to 1 Corinthians 15:1–3 she would have seen that there was a strong and coherent apostolic tradition guarded from the first by the followers of Jesus. And to suppose that the Roman Catholic church has suppressed women, when it gives such veneration to the Virgin Mary, is laughable, though it must be conceded that women are not given much of a voice in Roman Catholicism.

When she wrote her attractive book *The Gnostic Gospels*, as a young woman, Elaine Pagels showed a great deal of sympathy for the Gnostics, but some 20 years later when she wrote *Beyond Belief* she reveals how she had come to share their viewpoint. Alienated from evangelical Christianity when at high school – because someone told her that her Jewish friend who had died would go to hell – she nevertheless retained interest in the New Testament and made it the focus of her advanced studies. As we saw in Chapter Eight she had a moment of illumination while working on the *Gospel of Thomas* at Harvard. She came across the saying attributed there to Jesus: "If you bring forth what is within you, what you bring forth will save you." She loved this for two reasons. One, it did not tell her what to believe. Two, it enabled her to look to human potential for spiritual insight rather than to Jesus for salvation. As we saw, she does a careful comparison between the *Gospel of Thomas* and the Gospel of John. In John there is a close interrelation between the branch and the vine, the believer and the Lord. But in *Thomas* there is identification. The self is deified. That is the position that she has now adopted. It is no surprise that she confesses to being very enchanted by a woman who was the head of a Gnostic church in Palo Alto, and is interested in the blending of Christianity and Buddhism. She is not alone. This is a revival of the old pagan Pantheism and it is becoming very fashionable. It is the natural resting place for belief once the conviction of a transcendent Creator God is jettisoned.

It would be a great mistake to imagine that the reiterated sexual emphases in Brown the novelist and the serious scholars who stand behind him are merely an invitation to dogmatic feminism or free sex, though they include those elements. The main point of these revisionists is to advocate a faith very different from Christianity. It is Monism, the belief that all is essentially one and everything is embraced within the circle of this world – god, man, animals, sticks and stones. There is nothing else. Joseph Campbell, who influences George Lucas, the director of *Star Wars*, put it crisply: "In religions where the god or creator is the mother, the world is her body. There is nowhere else." And despite all the comforting imagery of the Mother Goddess from whom everything emerges and to whom everything returns, she is no personal God but an implacable life force. The "sacred feminine" is a giant con for the gullible. Monism offers us nothing but a blind impersonal force that animates everything. If you like to think of it this way, both paganism and Christianity offer us good news. Paganism offers liberation from the Creator to do your own thing, and save yourself. Christianity proposes reconciliation with the Creator to love and please him. They are irreconcilable.

And that is why it is worth returning to our earlier discussion of the kissing incident in the *Gospels of Mary* and *Philip*. It is profoundly significant. It is not about feminine leadership. It is not about eroticism. It is about the source of revelation. Does it come from our own inner beings or from outside, from God? As we saw, the Gnostics, who argued for secret revelations as the basis of their faith, liked to portray themselves as the downtrodden female (Mary) being abused by the chauvinistic catholic male (Peter). That is what the incident was all about. It was a struggle for determining the meaning of Christianity. Was its content to be defined by the New Testament Scriptures of apostolic origin, or by secret revelations to which the Gnostics laid claim? The church suppressed these books, and the whole Gnostic system from which they came, because in the final analysis they represented an entirely different and hostile religion to that revealed in the New Testament.

The church was right to suppress them – if suppress is the right word. To begin with, the Fathers denounced this Gnostic material. Then they made it clear that you could not mix poison and honey. And by the time of Athanasius it was appropriate to tell the church at large that such books were not to be countenanced among believers. "They are the invention of the heretics, who write according to their own will," said Athanasius. And that was probably the signal for the community that owned the Gnostic gospels to bury them in the sands near Nag Hammadi. For these Gnostic gospels really advocated salvation of the randomly elect few through knowledge, not the salvation available to all men and women the world over, through the death and resurrection of Jesus Christ. These were completely different religions. We have no reason to bemoan the demise of Gnosticism in the early centuries, and no cause to resurrect it in today's church and society. It has nothing to offer us.

Chapter Fourteen

Ⓣhe Ⓗeart of the Ⓜatter

T he purpose of this book has not primarily been to criticise *The Da Vinci Code*, although Brown's book was the occasion for my own. I have set out instead to show how rotten are the Gnostic foundations on which its main thesis stands, and how fallacious is the world view it propounds. For though in due course *The Da Vinci Code* will be forgotten, the world view of Naturalism which it embodies is perennial. But the spirituality it advocates is not true and it does not satisfy.

Despite its remarkable popularity, Brown's best-seller is full of errors. This has been demonstrated by conservative and liberal critics alike, particularly in Ben Witherington, *The Gospel Code*, Darrell Bock, *Breaking the Da Vinci Code* and James Garlow and Peter Jones, *Cracking Da Vinci's Code*. Brown is spectacularly wrong in much of what he asserts, and this is all the more reprehensible in the light of his claim at the very start of his novel that "all descriptions of artwork, architecture, documents and secret rituals in this novel are accurate."

This is simply not the case. It is not true that Jesus' divinity was decided (and by a narrow vote!) at the Council of Nicaea. It is not true that the Gnostic gospels predate the New Testament. It is not true that the contents of the New Testament were selected to serve Constantine's political agenda, or that 80 gospels were considered for inclusion in the New Testament. It is not true that Mary Magdalene was the leader on whom a feminist Christ intended to build his church. It is not true that "any gospels that described the earthly aspects of Jesus's life had to be omitted from the Bible" and that the Gnostic gospels were "excluded from the canon because they speak of Christ's ministry in very human terms" (has he ever studied the four biblical Gospels, I wonder, which are persistently and profoundly interested in earthly details?) In point of fact, the Gnostic gospels that he likes so much originate no earlier than the late second century. They favour an extreme dualism between spirit and body and have no interest in the historical Jesus, but are a bizarre collection of surreal secret sayings. The Dead Sea Scrolls make no reference to Jesus and the Nag Hammadi documents do not tell the story of the Grail! One might add that serious art historians do not consider the person next to Jesus in Leonardo's *The Last Supper* to be Mary Magdalene, that the Church did not burn five million witches in the Middle Ages – though its record is scarcely creditable. The Priory of Zion is not a mediaeval institution with a membership including Leonardo, Victor Hugo, Boyle and Newton, but first appeared in France in the late 1950s! And so one might go on. This book, which claims accuracy on matters of fact, is a farrago of factual errors.

Why then is it so popular? The mix of wicca, goddess worship, secret rituals and societies, symbolism, violence, murder, ancient lore in modern dress and a fast-moving detective story, with a new twist to an ancient quest for the Holy Grail – all this has made the book a great page-turner.

But the sub-plot, a subtle response to the current aversion to Christianity but hunger for spirituality, is what makes it so very trendy. Down with the Vatican and all its corruption and deception! Down with the Gospels and the deity of Christ! Down with the authoritarianism that has marked a male-dominated church! Let's replace it with an all-inclusive neo-paganism, where the sacred feminine comes into its own, where nobody is told what to believe, where all religions are much the same, and where nature worship with full sexual permissiveness is on the agenda. All of this is very attractive in today's society. And Brown's claim to factual accuracy, playing on the contemporary tendency to confuse fact with fiction, makes this a dangerous book. The danger is all the more real because of the prodigious ignorance of Christianity and its credentials among the population at large, and the almost complete lack of attractive Christian apologetic since the days of C.S. Lewis and Lesslie Newbigin.

What gives Brown's book a profound significance is the world view he advocates, which is shared, consciously or unconsciously, by millions in our day. It regards Christianity as outdated and based on error and deception, and exalts the worship of nature in its place. The heroine in Brown's story is the French cryptologist Sophie Neveu. Brown is forever using codes in this novel, and her names hint at ancient Wisdom (*sophia*), which is nevertheless new (*nouveau*). She is intended to be an example for the reader. At the outset she knows nothing of the "truth" but by the end of the story she is increasingly aware of this "new wisdom", which, as we have seen, is not new at all. It is a combination of ancient pagan goddess worship and Gnostic myths.

It has been necessary in this book to examine with some care the grounds upon which Christianity is built. These are the apostolic writings, embodying as they do the teaching of Jesus, the accounts of his death and resurrection, and the testimony of the eyewitness generation to him. We have seen that their writings were accorded immediate and lasting honour in the Christian community from the start. We have seen that nothing written after 140 AD was ever even considered for the canon of Scripture, and that there was remarkable agreement about which books indicated divine inspiration, came from the apostolic age, were orthodox in content and were widely recognised and useful in the post-apostolic church worldwide.

This enquiry has of necessity been wide-ranging and detailed. It has shown us that the Gnostic material upon which Brown and others base their novels is without exception much later than the New Testament writings, and is based on a spiritual world view entirely alien to that of Christianity. But the purpose of our study has not been merely to show that we can rely on the New Testament as we have received it. It has not merely been to undermine the facile trust which many film-makers, novelists and a few scholars seem to place in the Gnostic material. But it has been to reveal what is really happening in the massive adulation accorded to Dan Brown's book.

I want people to see that his purpose is to attack Christianity as a falsehood and to advocate nature mysticism or worship in its place. He hopes to replace theism with Monism. The Age of Aquarius, beloved of New Age and neo-pagan spirituality, has replaced the Age of Pisces, which was dominated, to a large extent, by a Christian world view. Since the 1960s the advocates of the new paganism have established new and radical views of the family, education, morals, marriage, sex, spirituality and God. The time has come, they feel, to sing the song of the "sacred feminine". In Dan Brown they have found a modern singer to proclaim it to a mass audience. The song includes the unity of all faiths, the erosion of the concept of sin, and the blending of religious and moral opposites into one androgynous whole – syncretism. "My hope for *The Da Vinci Code*", writes Brown in his website, "was that in addition to entertaining people that (*sic!*) it might

serve as an open door for readers to begin their own explo-
rations and rekindle their interest in topics of faith." Well, he
has certainly done that, and on an almost unparalleled scale.
But the faith he is encouraging people into is a pick'n'mix of
mysticism, with no transcendent deity, but with ancient goddess worship, gnosticism and sexual permissiveness. It is a
faith that sees this world as all there is, so we had better make
the most of it.

There are actually only two paths we can take among all
the religions of the world. One is to worship Nature, the other
to worship the Creator of Nature. As the apostle Paul put it,
you either worship "the creation" or else "the Creator – who
is blessed for ever" (Romans 1:25). I have written this book to
point up that choice. I wanted to attack the facile credulity
among thousands of undiscerning readers that *The Da Vinci
Code* has destroyed Christianity. I wanted to encourage a
healthy scepticism about sceptical positions like that of
Brown. I wanted to show the solidity of the evidence on which
the Christian faith and its documents are based, and how
shaky are the grounds on which novelties like *The Da Vinci
Code* are founded. Let Charles Haddon Spurgeon, that great
defender of the faith in a previous generation, have the last
word: "Nowadays they cry 'Eureka!, Eureka!', as if they had
found a new truth; yet they have not discovered a diamond,
but a piece of broken glass!"

Who's Who and What's What

Acts of John: imaginative and strongly docetic Gnostic work from the end of the second century.

Acts of Paul and Thecla: a romance concerning Paul and a female admirer, written about 170 AD. Its author was dismissed from office for forging it under the name of Paul.

Acts of Peter: an apocryphal work closely parallel to the *Acts of John*. Written in the second century, it enjoyed a considerable readership among both orthodox and heretical Christians well into the fourth century.

Apocalypse of Peter: a fairly early second-century apocryphal book of revelations embracing pagan ideas of heaven and hell, which influenced Dante's *Inferno*. It is only partially extant in two very different forms. Much read in the early church.

Apocalypse of Paul: a third-century development of the *Apocalypse of Peter*, it was found in the buried library at Nag Hammadi and describes Paul's ascents through the various heavens beloved of the Gnostics.

Apocryphon of John: a second-century Gnostic work, featuring, among a bizarre and complex cosmogeny, Jesus and Sophia (Divine Wisdom) as emanations from the supreme God of light.

Aquila: an early-second-century Jewish proselyte who translated the Hebrew Scriptures into Greek afresh, since the Christians had "stolen" the Septuagint translation.

Archons: fabled celestial beings in the Gnostic systems, somewhat analogous to angels.

Arius: an influential early-fourth-century leader who claimed Jesus was not completely God. His views were condemned at the Council of Nicaea in AD 325.

Athanasius: a fourth-century bishop of Alexandria and champion of orthodoxy over against Arianism.

Augustine: (354–430 AD) became one of the greatest saints and theologians of the church, after a non-Christian youth. His *City of God* remained one of the most significant books for a thousand years.

Basilides: lived in Alexandria from 117–138 AD. He wrote extensively but his works are lost. Irenaeus and Hippolytus give different accounts of his teaching, which was strongly Gnostic.

Canon: a word that means reed or measuring stick and as such is the standard of orthodoxy. The word is also used of a collection of sacred books.

Carpocrates: a second-century Gnostic from Alexandria who practised magic and gross immorality.

Cerinthus: late-first-century proto-Gnostic who denied that the historical Jesus was the Christ. The Johannine letters are probably directed against him.

Clement of Alexandria: (c. 150–215 AD) head of the great Christian School in Alexandria. Highly educated in Greek culture and Scripture and sought to combine the two without becoming Gnostic.

Church Fathers: a shorthand way of referring to orthodox Christian writers between the second and fourth centuries.

Constantine: the first Christian Emperor (274–337 AD), who summoned the Council of Nicaea and was a friend of Bishop Eusebius of Caesarea.

Coptic: the normal Egyptian language from the third to the tenth centuries AD. The Gnostic texts were mostly written in Coptic.

Demiurge: an inferior god in Gnostic thought who created the (fallen) earth. The word means "people-maker".

Diatessaron: the combination of our four Gospels into a continuous narrative, by Tatian about 160 AD. The name means "through the four" and its publication is a notable witness to the authority already enjoyed by the four Gospels.

Didache or *Teaching of the Twelve Apostles*: probably dates from the end of the first century. It is a short early Christian treatise on morals and church life. Its author is unknown.

Dionysius of Corinth: late-second-century bishop.

Docetism: the belief that the divine Christ only *seemed* to be human and only *seemed* to suffer.

Dualism: belief in the complete distinction between the purity of the immaterial world and the corruption of the material world.

Encratites: a group of ascetic second-century sects which renounced marriage, meat and wine. They took asceticism to extremes and many of them were Gnostic and produced the Apocryphal gospels and Acts.

Epiphanius: (315–403 AD) Bishop of Salamis, an orthodox supporter of monasticism, who wrote the *Panarion*, or *Refutation of all heresies*, which though poorly constructed and repetitive has much useful historical material.

Epistle of Barnabas: an orthodox early-second-century text claiming the Old Testament and its promises for Christians. Some Christians read it alongside Scripture, thinking (wrongly) that it was written by Barnabas, the companion of St Paul.

Epistle of Clement: Clement, a much-respected Christian leader (perhaps bishop) at Rome, wrote to the Corinthians in 96 AD a letter deploring their dismissal of their leaders. It was read alongside Scripture in some places, perhaps believing that it was written by the Clement in the New Testament (Philippians 4:3).

Eusebius: (269–339 AD) Bishop of Caesarea in Palestine. A friend of Constantine, he wrote the first church history since Luke, known as the *Ecclesiastical History*. It is invaluable to us as an informed record of the previous two centuries. He exercised an important influence at Nicaea.

Gnostics: a pseudo-Christian variety of sects in the second to fourth centuries, most of whom who believed that the god of creation was not the pure supreme God, and that there was a distinction between the Jesus who died on the cross and the transcendent Christ. They believed that their hidden revelation was superior to anything the "Great Church" had to offer, and provided them with a *gnosis* or knowledge which gave them salvation.

Great Church: a convenient name for catholic or orthodox Christians in their struggle against Gnosticism.

Gospel of Barnabas: a fourteenth-century forgery, written in Italian by a native of Italy who had renounced Christianity for Islam.

Secret Gospel of Mark: not our Mark but a disputed fragment of a seventeenth-century page, which may have come from the second century, and adapted the canonical Mark in the direction of magic initiation rites and homosexuality.

Gospel of Mary (of Magdala): a Gnostic gospel probably written in the late second century, which claimed Jesus loved Mary and gave her secret revelations, hidden from the male disciples.

Gospel of Philip: a Gnostic gospel of the early third century which regarded Mary as a favourite disciple, often kissed by Jesus.

Gospel of Thomas: a mid-second-century Gnostic gospel, composed entirely of 114 sayings, some of which may be genuine sayings of Jesus, but the material as a whole is definitely Gnostic.

Gospel according to the Hebrews: a mid-second-century gospel popular among Hebrew Christians, known only in fragmentary citations.

Gospel of the Egyptians: a late-second-century Gnostic gospel written for the Encratites, people who rejected marriage and favoured the elimination of sexual differences in a "unisex" direction.

Gospel of Peter: a Jewish Christian gospel from the middle of the second century, which is aware of all our four Gospels and displays docetic tendencies.

Gospel of Truth: found in Coptic at Nag Hammadi, possibly the work of the second-century heresiarch Valentinus. The world originates in the fall of Sophia (Wisdom), whose offspring the Demiurge is the God of the Old Testament, rejected by the Gnostics. The author divides humans into *pneumatikoi* (spiritual people – the Gnostics!), *psychikoi* (soulish or unenlightened church members) and the rest of mankind, *hulikoi* (made of matter and headed for perdition). This second-century work quotes most of our New Testament, no doubt to aid its credibility.

Heresy: the choice of theological positions incompatible with the New Testament.

Hippolytus: (170–235 AD) a major scholar at Rome. Wrote a *Refutation of All Heresies* in ten volumes, and an important manual on church order, *The Apostolic Tradition*.

Ignatius: (c. 35–107 AD), early Bishop of Antioch of whom little is known until he went to Rome earnestly seeking martyrdom (to be killed by wild beasts). On the way he wrote important letters to seven churches, which are extant. They include quotations from much of what became our New Testament.

Irenaeus: (c. 130–200) was the principal proponent of orthodoxy against Gnostic systems in the second century, and the most significant Christian controversialist before Origen. His surviving five-volume work *Against Heresies* (for which his own name was *An Exposure and Refutation of Knowledge (gnosis) that is Falsely So-Called*) is invaluable for understanding the complexities of second-century orthodoxy and heresy.

Jamnia: a city near Joppa where an important rabbinic gathering was held about 85 AD, partly to determine the right of certain books to remain in the Old Testament canon.

Jerome: (c. 342–420) an ascetic Christian monk of enormous learning. Translated the Greek Bible into Latin.

Justin Martyr: a second-century Christian philosopher who wrote against Marcion, c. 150 AD. His key surviving works are the *Dialogue with Trypho* and the *First* and *Second Apologies*.

Marcion: (c. 100–160) an influential heretical teacher who rejected the Old Testament and formed a canon of an abridged Gospel of Luke and the epistles of Paul. Had some Gnostic affinities, and was a major threat to the orthodox.

Millenarianism: the belief, common in the second century, that there would be a period of a thousand years of Christ's reign on earth before the End.

Montanus: a mid-second-century ecstatic and charismatic teacher who regarded his own revelations as authoritative. Very influential.

Nag Hammadi: place in the Egyptian desert where a fourth-century Gnostic library, comprising 52 texts in Coptic, was unearthed in 1945 AD.

Nicaea: a church council convened in 325 AD to discuss the definition of the deity of Christ and to banish Arianism.

Origen: (c. 185–254) a distinguished theologian who led the great Christian educational School at Alexandria and dealt comprehensively with heretical views, particularly of the sceptic Celsus.

Orthodox: a term that refers to true belief based on the apostolic documents.

Pagan: someone who can worship many gods or none – often a nature worshipper in some form.

Panentheism: the belief that the universe shares the nature of God, who nevertheless is not confined to it.

Pantheism: the belief that God and the universe are identical.

Pantaenus: a convert from Stoicism who lived in the last half of the second century. He founded the great Catechetical School at Alexandria, led his successor, Clement, to faith, and then went as a missionary to India.

Papias: (c. 60–130) Bishop of Hierapolis, the disciple of John and companion of Polycarp and an important, if enigmatic, early witness to Jesus and the apostles. His *Expositions of the Oracles of the Lord* has perished apart from some citations.

Philo: (c. 20 BC to 50 AD) very important Jewish writer and exegete in Alexandria, who treated the Old Testament allegorically.

Plato: (c. 429–347 BC) the Athenian philosopher who has profoundly influenced all classical culture and Western thought.

Pleroma: a word that means "fulness" denoting the angels and other personified ideas and heavenly beings that go to make up the supreme transcendent God worshipped by the Gnostics.

Polycarp: (c. 69–155) Bishop of Smyrna and leading figure in Asia. He strongly opposed the Marcionites and Valentinians. His *Letter to the Philippians* is delightful and quotes extensively from the apostolic writings, showing how highly they were venerated at a very early stage. He was burnt alive in 155 AD after refusing to deny Christ.

Second Treatise of the Great Seth: third-century Gnostic work, in the form of a revelatory dialogue. It is docetic and denies that the Jesus who dies on the cross is the Christ.

Shepherd of Hermas: an orthodox, if strange, early Christian book written before 150 AD.

Simon Magus: the pseudo-Christian recorded in Acts 8 who became a very early and influential Gnostic and magician.

Tatian: a mid-second-century student of Justin Martyr who was a Christian apologist but later became the founder of an ascetic sect, the Encratites. He wrote the *Diatessaron*, combining the four accounts of the Gospels into one narrative, which was used in the Syrian Church until the fifth century.

Tertullian: a vigorous anti-Gnostic writer (c. 160–220) whose rigorist views led him to Montanism. He was the first Christian theologian to write in Latin rather than Greek.

For Further Reading

The Ante-Nicene Fathers: Translations of the Writings of the Fathers Down to 325 AD, ed. Roberts and Donaldson, Eerdmans, 1987.

The Holy Blood and The Holy Grail, by Michael Baigent, Richard Leigh and Henry Lincoln, Doubleday, 1982.

The Da Vinci Code, by Dan Brown, Bantam, 2003.

Breaking the Da Vinci Code, by Darrell Bock, Nelson, 2004.

Cracking Da Vinci's Code, by James L. Garlow and Peter Jones, Victor, 2004.

The Gospel Code, by Ben Witherington, IVP, 2004.

The Four Gospels and the One Gospel of Jesus Christ, by Martin Hengel, Trinity Press International, 2000.

Lord Jesus Christ: Devotion to Jesus in Earliest Christianity, by Larry W. Hurtado, Eerdmans, 2003.

Hidden Gospels: How the Search for Jesus Lost its Way, by Philip Jenkins, OUP, 2001.

Lost Christianities, by Bart Ehrman, OUP, 2003.

The Gospel of Mary of Magdala: Jesus and the First Woman Apostle, by Karen King, Polebridge Press, 2003.

Ancient Christian Gospels, by Helmut Koester, Trinity Press International, 1990.

The Canon of the New Testament, by Bruce Metzger, Clarendon, 1987.

The Canon of Scripture, by F.F. Bruce, IVP, 1988.

The Gnostic Gospels, by Elaine Pagels, Weidenfeld and Nicholson, 1980.

Beyond Belief: The Secret Gospel of Thomas, by Elaine Pagels, Random House, 2003.

The Nag Hammadi Library (in translation), by James M. Robinson, 1988.

Gnosis: The Nature and History of Gnosticism, by Kurt Rudolph, Harper and Row, 1987.

Irenaeus of Lyons, by Robert Grant, Routledge, 1997.

The Early Church, by Henry Chadwick, Penguin, 1967.

Apocryphal Gospels, by Hans-Josef Klauck, T. and T. Clark International, 2003.

Who was Jesus? by N.T. Wright, SPCK, 1992.

The Resurrection of the Son of God, by N.T. Wright, SPCK, 2003.

The Spirit and the Letter: Studies in the Biblical Canon, by John Barton, SPCK, 1997.

Clement of Alexandria and a Secret Gospel of Mark, by Morton Smith, Harvard University Press, 1973.

Jesus the Magician, by Morton Smith, Harper and Row, 1978.

Four Other Gospels, by John Dominic Crossan, Winston Press, 1985.

Unity and Diversity in the New Testament, by J.D.G. Dunn, SCM Press, 1977.